ELECTORAL SYST
OF CONSUME1

M000302958

This book investigates the effects of electoral systems on the relative legislative and, hence, regulatory influence of competing interests in society. Building on Ronald Rogowski and Mark Kayser's extension of the classic Stigler-Peltzman model of regulation, the authors demonstrate that majoritarian electoral arrangements should empower consumers relative to producers. Employing real price levels as a proxy for consumer power, the book rigorously establishes this proposition over time, within the OECD, and across a large sample of developing countries. Majoritarian electoral arrangements depress real prices by approximately ten percent, all else equal. The authors carefully construct and test their argument and broaden it to consider the overall welfare effects of electoral system design and the incentives of actors in the choice of electoral institutions.

Eric C. C. Chang is Associate Professor of Political Science at Michigan State University. He studies comparative political economy, political institutions, political corruption, and democratization in developed and developing democracies. His publications have appeared in multiple journals including the *Journal of Politics, British Journal of Political Science, World Politics, Comparative Political Studies,* and *European Journal of Political Research.*

Mark Andreas Kayser is Professor of Applied Quantitative Methods and Comparative Politics at the Hertie School of Governance in Berlin. His research focuses on the comparative and international political economy of elections. His work has appeared in journals including the *American Journal of Political Science, American Political Science Review, British Journal of Political Science,* and *European Journal of Political Research.*

Drew A. Linzer is Assistant Professor of Political Science at Emory University. His research explores patterns of public opinion and voting behavior in democracies around the world, and their consequences for political representation and quality of governance. His work has appeared in journals including the *Journal of Politics, World Politics, Political Analysis,* and *Journal of Statistical Software.*

Ronald Rogowski is Professor of Political Science at UCLA. His book, *Commerce and Coalitions,* received the American Political Science Association's prize for best book in political economy. He is a former member of the National Science Foundation's Political Science Panel and currently chairs one of the European Research Council's Social Sciences Panels. He is also lead editor of the *American Political Science Review.*

Cambridge Studies in Comparative Politics

General Editor
Margaret Levi *University of Washington, Seattle*

Assistant General Editors
Kathleen Thelen *Massachusetts Institute of Technology*
Erik Wibbels *Duke University*

Associate Editors
Robert H. Bates *Harvard University*
Stephen Hanson *University of Washington, Seattle*
Torben Iversen *Harvard University*
Stathis Kalyvas *Yale University*
Peter Lange *Duke University*
Helen Milner *Princeton University*
Frances Rosenbluth *Yale University*
Susan Stokes *Yale University*

Other Books in the Series

David Austen-Smith, Jeffry A. Frieden, Miriam A. Golden, Karl Ove Moene, and Adam Przeworski, eds., *Selected Works of Michael Wallerstein: The Political Economy of Inequality, Unions, and Social Democracy*
Andy Baker, *The Market and the Masses in Latin America: Policy Reform and Consumption in Liberalizing Economies*
Lisa Baldez, *Why Women Protest: Women's Movements in Chile*

Series list continues after the Index.

Electoral Systems and the Balance of Consumer-Producer Power

Eric C. C. Chang

Michigan State University

Mark Andreas Kayser

Hertie School of Governance, Berlin

Drew A. Linzer

Emory University

Ronald Rogowski

University of California, Los Angeles

CAMBRIDGE
UNIVERSITY PRESS

CAMBRIDGE UNIVERSITY PRESS
Cambridge, New York, Melbourne, Madrid, Cape Town, Singapore,
São Paulo, Delhi, Dubai, Tokyo, Mexico City

Cambridge University Press
32 Avenue of the Americas, New York, NY 10013-2473, USA

www.cambridge.org
Information on this title: www.cambridge.org/9780521138154

© Eric C. C. Chang, Mark Andreas Kayser, Drew A. Linzer, and Ronald Rogowski
2011

First published 2011

Printed in the United States of America

A catalog record for this publication is available from the British Library.

Library of Congress Cataloging in Publication data

Electoral systems and the balance of consumer-producer power /
Eric C. C. Chang ... [et al.].
p. cm. – (Cambridge studies in comparative politics)
Includes bibliographical references and index.
ISBN 978-0-521-19265-1 (hardback)
1. Elections – Economic aspects. 2. Voting – Economic aspects.
3. Consumers. 4. Prices. 5. Comparative government. I. Chang, Eric C. C.,
1971– II. Title. III. Series
JF1001.E475 2010
339 – dc22 2010018291

ISBN 978-0-521-19265-1 Hardback
ISBN 978-0-521-13815-4 Paperback

Contents

Acknowledgments

Perhaps like many books, this one was long in the making. It began in 1999 as a paper by Ronald Rogowski and Mark Kayser on the effect of industrial concentration on the clout of various sectors in securing favors from the U.S. Congress. They used sectoral price deviations from a world average to measure "clout" and soon became interested in price-levels themselves. That paper was never published but the "price papers" by the authors in this book appeared three times in print before taking the form seen here.

Over the eleven years in which this book took shape, life marched on for all of us. Perhaps unlike other volumes, parts of this one were written on three continents and eight cities – Los Angeles, Oxford, Rochester, East Lansing, Berkeley, Atlanta, Taipei, and Berlin. Three of the authors got married and four children were born: Clare Rogowski, Ryan Chang, Cleo Linzer, and Milena Sophie Kayser.

A project such as this one accumulates a lot of debts. We owe our gratitude to a long list of people who have patiently read draft chapters or questioned us at conferences. It is difficult to assemble the full list of names of those whose comments pushed us along but we would like to thank explicitly the following people whose insight in some way improved this book: Kathleen Bawn, Gary Cox, Daniel Diermeier, Robert Franzese, Jeffry Frieden, Daniel Ho, Torben Iversen, Mark Jones, David Karol, Jonathan Katz, Ed Leamer, John Londregan, Bing Powell, Ross Schaap, David Soskice, Michael Thies, and Taehee Whang.

Various chapters have been presented in multiple fora. In addition to those listed above, we are grateful for the

Acknowledgments

comments we received from participants at the UCLA Working Group on Efficient Institutions; the fall 2001 meeting of the Research Group on Political Institutions and Economic Policy at Harvard; Yale's Leitner Political Economy Seminar Series; the Political Science Seminar at Nuffield College, Oxford; the IPE Seminar at the University of Southern California; the Political Science Seminar at Penn State University; the Institute of Political Science at Academia Sinica; and various annual meetings of the American Political Science Association. Leah Halvorson deserves special acknowledgment for coordinating much of our effort and several meetings in Los Angeles. We thank Dayna Sadow for her diligence and good judgment in drafting the index. We are also grateful to several research assistants, particularly Patrick Lam and Louis Coiffait. Peter Katsirubas at Aptara kept us on schedule, as much as possible, with the final assembly and production; and the editors and the good people at Cambridge University Press, especially Lewis Bateman and Anne Lovering Rounds, made this all possible.

Most importantly, we thank our wives and families for their boundless patience and inspiration. Eric would like to express his greatest appreciation to his wife, Shufen Chao, for relieving him from baby duty even though it was obvious to her that her husband did not work on the book all the time. Mark met his future wife, Daniela, one year after this project began and could not have been as happy and productive without her. Drew is grateful as always to his wife Rachel for her support, perspective, and encouragement. Ron's wife, Karin Best, and his daughters Emma and Clare Rogowski, spent the crucial year in Berlin, learning German and putting up with his long work hours on this book and another one.

1

Introduction

"People of the same trade seldom meet together, ... but the conversation ends in a conspiracy against the public, or in some contrivance to raise prices." [I.x.]

"Consumption is the sole end and purpose of all production. ... But ... the interest of the consumer is almost constantly sacrificed to that of the producer." [IV.viii.]

Adam Smith, *The Wealth of Nations*

Even casual tourists – perhaps especially casual tourists – immediately notice one major difference among the countries they visit: *prices vary*. The restaurant meal that would cost $50 in Los Angeles can be had for $15 in Ensenada but will lighten one's wallet by $200 in Tokyo. More astonishingly, what appear to be identical and fully tradable goods – a writing tablet, a package of brand-name diapers – retails for far more in Norway than in Spain, or – as some pioneering economic field studies have shown (Engel and Rogers 2001) – for far more on one side of the street (which happens to lie in

Switzerland and accepts only Swiss francs) than on the other (which is in France and accepts only Euros).

The person who actually moves to another country, and lives and works there for some time, notices another striking difference: *levels of regulation vary.* Whoever attempts to build a house, open a business, buy an automobile, or even change her address will find the process easy (or perhaps scarcely regulated at all) in some countries, but subject to repeated licensure and inspections in others.

Cross-border managers or investors will be struck by three other salient contrasts: *market competition, incentives to innovate,* and *service-sector efficiency* differ greatly across countries. In Britain or the United States (so at least the conventional wisdom has it), firms compete vigorously in most sectors, concentration and market power are limited, and shareholders are powerful. Hostile takeovers of underperforming firms are commonplace. In Germany or Japan, or more generally in the "organized" market economies (see, e.g., Hall and Soskice 2001), cross-holdings of shares and board seats, direct involvement of major banks, and sheer market concentration lead to muted competition and weak shareholders: hostile takeovers occasion astonishment and rarely succeed. Relatedly, *cost-cutting innovations* – computerized publishing, Wal-Mart-style retailing, Web-based retailing – are accepted rapidly in most "Anglo-American" economies but are often resisted tenaciously on the European continent.

Introduction

Finally, acute social observers – whether tourists, residents, or scholars – will notice vast differences in *social and economic inequality* among countries. In Sweden, Finland, or even Germany, one encounters little of either the dire poverty or the wretched excess to which Americans have grown oblivious; but even Americans can be shocked by the inequalities they encounter in places like Mexico or Russia.[1]

Admittedly much of this variation can be explained simply by countries' circumstances: poorer countries have lower prices and more inequality, smaller countries will have more concentrated industries because fewer firms can achieve minimum efficient scale, authoritarian states will regulate more (and, usually, more arbitrarily). However, with all of those factors considered, a lot of variation will remain unexplained: countries that are similar in wealth, size, democracy, and even history will differ markedly in prices, regulation, competition, and equality.

In this book, we contend (a) that these variations are systematically related, and (b) that much of the otherwise

---

[1] The Luxembourg Incomes Study (LIS) now permits reliable comparisons among countries on such standard measures of inequality as the Gini index. Where zero represents total equality of incomes and one total inequality, in the period 1995–2000 Finland stood at .23, Sweden at .24, Germany at .25; Italy and the UK were at .34, the United States at .37, Russia at .44, Mexico at .49. Perhaps more vividly, in Norway the top decile earned 2.8 times what the bottom decile did; in the United States, that ratio was 5.5; in Mexico, 10.4. See www.lisproject.org/keyfigures/ineqtable.htm.

3

unexplained variation may be attributed to differences in political institutions, specifically – at least among the world's democracies – to the *kind of electoral system they employ*.[2]

The systematic relation is this: Countries have higher prices – again, controlling for other factors – in large part because their extensive regulations restrain competition and sustain oligopoly power. Weak competition, in turn, permits entrenched interests to resist innovation. Perhaps paradoxically, but particularly in a globalizing economy under wage pressure from third-world imports and outsourcing, monopoly power and resistance to innovation preserve traditional high-wage jobs and thus make for greater social equality. Less obviously, but quite intuitively, these protective arrangements inflict deadweight welfare losses. The economy produces less overall than it could, so the overall effect is to divide a smaller pie more equally. Thus, we expect the same countries to have high prices, weak competition, extensive regulation, sluggish innovation, lowered productivity, and comparatively high social equality.

Politics and political institutions enter the picture this way: high prices, weak competition, and regulatory barriers

---

[2] This is not to deny that the electoral system itself may be endogenous (a possibility we entertain at greater length in Chapter 6), or that it may work through additional channels. It is to affirm, as we find consistently, that a change in electoral system almost invariably has strong price effects.

to entry flow largely from governmental policies that favor producers or business firms. The triumph of such policies under some governments reveals a fundamental political fact about them, namely that producers are politically much stronger than consumers are. Producers can be politically stronger for many reasons, but political institutions are among the most important factors. The institutions that matter are the rules and conventions that translate citizen preferences into choices of leaders: in democracies, we look particularly at the electoral "rules" by which votes decide the allocation of parliamentary seats and executive offices. Our basic insight is just this: the more that a marginal shift in citizen preferences matters for the fate of political leaders – or, confining ourselves to democracies, the higher the seats-votes elasticity of the given electoral system – the more policy will be biased toward consumers (and away from producers). In addition, one sign of that bias, at least in countries with effective institutions, will be lower real prices, as political leaders restrain the cartels and regulations that permit producers to extract quasi-monopolistic rents.

The general logic behind our theory is as follows. Elected governments generate regulatory policies that broadly influence the costs to producers of manufacturing a wide array of goods. To the extent that regulations distort markets away from perfect competition, they also affect the prices producers may charge for the goods they produce. In short, regulations play a significant role in determining both producer profits and consumer prices. The problem for politicians, who desire to maximize their political and electoral support from both producers *and* consumers, is that these two factors are quite at odds. Producers, of course, desire greater profits while consumers desire lower prices. Politicians must therefore mediate between these two conflicting preferences when devising regulatory policy. In the event that consumers are stronger than producers are, politicians will respond by setting policies that engender lower prices for consumers – but also lower profits for producers. Where and when producers are stronger than consumers, politicians will set policies that lead to higher profits for producers (at least in the short run) – but also higher prices for consumers. Strength, here, is equivalent to political power, and the regulatory policies that governments set reflect the relative power of these two constituencies.

What determines the comparative political strength of producers versus consumers is chiefly[3] the *electoral system* though which the interests of both groups are aggregated and expressed. Electoral rules and institutions determine how votes are tabulated and translated into election outcomes:

---

[3] However, not only. As will be seen in the formal discussion of Chapter 2, the rules of campaign finance also matter, because producers can typically mobilize more money – indeed, in our stylized model, *only* producers can mobilize money (although they can also mobilize votes).

namely, which politicians and parties get elected, and in what proportion. By shaping the power differential between producers and consumers, different electoral systems create different incentives for politicians to regulate markets. Ultimately, the choice of electoral systems has a significant impact on countries' price levels. Variation between electoral systems, cross-nationally and over time, predicts variation in the real prices consumers pay for goods.

In particular (and as will be developed in far greater detail later), as electoral systems become increasingly "responsive" – that is to say, as small changes in vote shares produce increasingly large changes in seat shares – politicians will increasingly prioritize consumers' (i.e., voters) wishes over those of producers. All else equal, in majoritarian or single-member-district electoral systems, or where strong presidents are elected directly, consumers are relatively strong and prices will be comparatively low. On the other hand, in proportional parliamentary electoral systems – where the seats-votes relationship is, by design, approximately one-to-one – consumers are weaker, and as a result, prices will be comparatively high.

Responsiveness is a term to which we will return repeatedly in this text. Assessing the formal structures of a country's electoral system is but one way, albeit usually the most important one, of getting at this idea. Where, for whatever reason, one party regularly captures a lopsided majority of the electorate

(India under Congress Party domination, Japan in the heyday of the LDP, Mexico under the PRI hegemony, Northern Ireland under the Unionists), incumbents have little reason to fear voter discontent whatever the electoral system – and indeed, as we demonstrate in Chapter 2, voters in such circumstances may actually have higher impact under proportional electoral systems.

Even where such one-party, or "one-and-one-half party" (Scalapino and Massumi 1962), systems do not prevail, responsiveness diminishes to the extent that voters are locked in to partisan loyalties by ascriptive (ethnic, religious, regional, racial) ties. This is especially the case when homogenous blocs of voters are geographically concentrated within particular electoral districts. If Catholic voters will support the Catholic party as a statement of tribal loyalty, and regardless of that party's performance on specific issues, Catholic party leaders can be as unresponsive as they wish to rank-and-file sentiment. To the extent that most or all voters in a given society vote only their ascriptive loyalties (and hence, as one wag once said of mid-twentieth-century Switzerland, "The election returns are but the census in another form"), overall responsiveness will be low. Hence, in practice, we must look not only at the electoral system (both for parliament and, if one exists, for a strong presidency), but at (a) how *competitive* elections are and (b) how *ethnically polarized* voters are.

8

Introduction

That said, we return to our main point, which we argue in detail in the next chapter: that less responsive democracies will disadvantage consumers and impose higher real prices. Of course, our theory assumes, perhaps too implicitly, that institutions have effects; that governments actually govern. In what Huntington (1968) first called "weakly institutionalized" regimes, including ostensibly democratic ones, policy is chaotic, laws go unenforced, government revenues are insecure, and corruption is pervasive. Elected politicians often win votes by patronage rather than policy (Kitschelt and Wilkinson 2007). Is it possible that less developed countries (LDCs), or some subset of them, have particular properties that would negate our expectations about electoral-system effects? Certainly one can imagine that in economies that depend heavily on a few primary-product exports and import almost all consumer goods – in earlier periods, Chilean or Zambian copper, Argentine wheat and beef, Brazilian coffee – producers might paradoxically demand low prices (a devalued exchange rate), while consumers might agitate for an overvalued exchange rate (i.e., "high" prices; see again Bates 1997). Whether, in such circumstances, the exact form of the electoral system matters for regulation remains for us an open question, to be decided empirically rather than theoretically. As we find later (somewhat to our surprise), electoral systems have almost exactly the same effects in poorer as in richer democracies.

Plan of the Book

Chapter 2 states our theoretical argument, including a fuller development of the welfare implications and possible endogeneity of electoral systems. Chapter 3 offers a first empirical test, focusing on panel evidence from the advanced industrial economies between 1970 and 2000 – a period that, fortuitously, included some important changes in a few of the richer countries' electoral systems (with, happily for us, almost exactly the effects our argument would predict). We concentrate on these countries because of their longer democratic histories, the greater likelihood that their institutions affect outcomes, and their readier availability of reliable data. To put the matter more strongly: if the effect we predict did not show up here, and prevail also in over-time analysis, our theory would simply be wrong.

Chapter 4 greatly extends the empirical test to include all democracies – indeed, all extensive periods of democratic rule in all countries – between 1972 and 2000. While our theoretical argument explicitly foresaw the possibility that electoral systems would have weaker, or indeed perhaps opposite, effects in poorer democracies, we find that the impact of electoral systems on competitiveness and prices is almost identical. Hence what we intended as a somewhat daring extension turns out to be strong evidence of the theory's robustness – and, in our view, of the improbability that some alternative mechanism (e.g., the kind of centralized wage bargaining that prevails mostly in more advanced economies) explains enduring price differences. Broadening the sample of democratic countries from twenty-three in Chapter 3 to more than seventy-five in Chapter 4 also enables us to apply a different set of statistical models for the analysis of time-series cross-sectional data. In particular, in Chapter 4 we employ a generalized estimating equation approach rather than the OLS models used in Chapter 3, which makes it possible to model directly the time-dynamics of real price levels within countries. This method also better accommodates that so few countries, in practice, ever actually change electoral systems from proportional to majoritarian, or vice versa.

Because we know (and helpful critics have occasionally reminded us) that large-N studies can conceal important exceptions and can "black box" crucial mechanisms, in Chapter 5 we supplement our overall picture with a closer examination of mechanisms (including the link between electoral systems and barriers to entry) and two highly relevant case studies: the change(s) of electoral system in Italy in the 1990s, and the "vanishing marginals" in U.S. congressional elections in recent decades. What motivations were involved (particularly in the Italian case), and did the changes in these two cases have the predicted effects?

In Chapter 6, we enlarge on two aspects repeatedly mentioned at earlier points in the book, namely the ultimate endogeneity of electoral systems but, at the same time, their general "stickiness" or resistance to change. We offer an explanation for both that rests on the link between electoral systems and *economic inequality*. In brief, because inequality both sustains and is sustained by less responsive electoral systems – a point we argue in detail in Chapter 2 – countries tend to alter their methods of election only when some large exogenous shock (e.g., a major war) greatly increases or decreases inequality. Appropriate tests against historical data from the period between the two world wars support this hypothesis. Chapter 7 concludes, less with a summary of the argument than with a statement of further implications and future directions for research.

2

Electoral Systems and Consumer Power: Theoretical Considerations

We begin with some fundamental and still highly influential work on regulation and its effects by two leading economists of the mid-twentieth century, George Stigler and Sam Peltzman. We then move to develop a specific Stigler-Peltzman political support function and analyze the role of electoral responsiveness in it. We next consider possible welfare and distributional effects of regulated, high-price economic systems. We then consider how the analysis might differ in a small, open, export-dependent economy. Then, having analyzed the effect of various kinds of democratic constitutions, we consider some of the implications for nondemocracies, weakly institutionalized democracies, and less developed economies. Finally, we consider whether electoral systems can be regarded as exogenous and whether this affects our overall analysis.

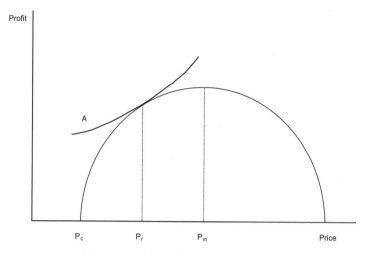

Figure 2.1. Stigler-Peltzman regulation

The Stigler-Peltzman Framework

The essential insight of the Stigler-Peltzman (S-P) analysis of regulation can be conveyed by a single and widely familiar diagram shown in Figure 2.1 (cf. Peltzman 1976, p. 224). Suppose that the price of a given industry's product is represented on the horizontal axis and its profits on the vertical one. At the perfectly competitive price (p_c), profits will be zero.[1] To the extent that regulation in any of its familiar forms – licensure schemes that artificially restrict supply, regulatory boards that set minimum prices, impediments to efficient retailing,

---

[1] Recall that, in a competitive market, price must equal cost of production (including the rent of capital). If a firm is charging more than that cost, hence making profits, some competitor can and will underbid it.

tariffs, quotas, and so on – raises the product's price above this competitive level, total industry profits begin to rise[2] until price reaches the level that a monopoly would impose; this is denoted as p_m.[3] If regulation becomes so restrictive of supply as to push price even beyond this monopolistic level, industry profits again decline, returning to zero (or even becoming negative) as the price becomes prohibitive.

Producers in this sector, of course, desire monopolistic price setting (p_m) while consumers prefer competitive pricing (p_c). Politicians, in the S-P framework, simply want to maximize support. They therefore consider the marginal rate of substitution between producer and consumer support, represented by a set of iso-support curves I_s, analogous to classic indifference curves. As politicians impose policies that increase profits, producers support those politicians more (higher contributions, a greater likelihood of voting for them). Yet the price increases that raise profits make consumers less likely to support those politicians. Similarly, regulations that decrease prices increase consumer support but decrease producer support. The iso-support curves describe the degree to which politicians can trade off or exchange consumer

---

[2] Absent barriers to entry, these profits will be competed away, but the same political power that imposes higher prices is usually adept enough to restrict entry.

[3] In classical analysis, this will be the point at which marginal cost just equals marginal revenue and industry profit is maximized.

support for producer support while maintaining a constant total level of combined support. In terms of the respective interests of producers and consumers, the iso-support curves express the extent to which increases or decreases in consumer prices must be counterbalanced, respectively, by decreases or increases in producer profits to maintain a constant level of political support. Moving along any given iso-support curve is equivalent to translating shifts in producer support (as determined by profits) into necessary counterbalancing shifts in consumer support (as determined by prices).

Concretely, suppose that a politician faces the situation depicted as point A in Figure 2.1: profits are high, prices low. The almost flat iso-support curve depicted at that point tells us that the politician can increase prices considerably without losing much consumer support, and will need to increase profits only slightly to gain offsetting producer support. As prices rise further, however – again, as shown in Figure 2.1 – consumers become more resistant: further rises lose more consumer support, and profits must rise more (the curve becomes steeper) to garner offsetting producer support.

Just as with indifference curves, we should imagine an infinity of iso-support curves, describing a kind of contour map of political support, increasing as we move to the northwest of the graph: that is, if the politician can both decrease prices and increase profits, support will unambiguously grow. Any particular iso-support curve is assumed to be convex from below for the same reason that obtains with indifference curves: the more one need (here, for example, consumer support) is already satisfied, the readier one is to sacrifice some of that good to gain a little of the other (here, producer support).

In this manner, any specific set of iso-support curves captures the electoral influence of consumers' interests vis-à-vis producers' interests on politicians. Iso-support curves are unique to a country's economic and political institutions – that is, we initially take them as given. Considering the balance of consumer and producer power, strategic politicians make regulatory decisions that maximize support from both camps. In equilibrium, politicians indirectly set prices at the highest point of tangency between the iso-support curves and the price-profit hump through the regulatory policies they implement. One hypothetical iso-support curve in its equilibrium position is depicted in Figure 2.1A.

The S-P theory predicts that government will bring price (and hence profits) to precisely the level indicated by the point of tangency, denoted here as p_r, the regulated price. To solidify this point, let us consider the iso-support curves (and the prices they yield) more closely. Imagine a world in which (for whatever reason) producers are quite powerful relative to consumers in a given sector. In this world, it takes a large *increase* in consumer support to compensate for a small *decrease* in producer support. Were profits to decrease even slightly – thus lowering producer support – prices would have

Electoral Systems and Balance of Consumer-Producer Power

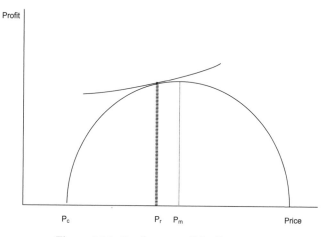

Figure 2.1A. Producers politically strong

to decrease by some quite large amount to compensate for this loss by an equivalent gain in consumer support. In terms of iso-support curves, this relationship would be described by a curve that is nearly flat (Fig. 2.1A). Logically enough, regulators impose (or enact restrictions that yield) almost the monopoly price p_m. Failing to do so would result in a nearly irreplaceable loss of producer support.

Conversely, if consumers greatly outweigh producers in a given sector, the iso-support curves will be almost vertical. The power of consumers in this alternate world is expressed in terms of the massive increases in profit politicians must award to producers (thus increasing producer support) to compensate for even slight price increases (which depress consumer support). Put another way, to compensate for the

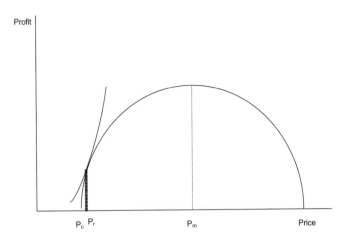

Figure 2.1B. Consumers politically strong

ire that even a slight price increase would arouse among consumers, profits would have to rise hugely. Naturally, politicians will depart very little from the competitive price p_c when presented with such a scenario. This situation is depicted in Figure 2.1B.

In this precise sense, price – or, more exactly, departure from competitive price once we have controlled for other relevant factors[4] – indicates the balance of consumer-producer political power in a given industry.[5]

---

[4] As Chapters 3 and 4 make clear, we build on existing literatures that relate countries' real prices to (*inter alia*) their per capita wealth, their exposure to world markets, and the size of their home markets.

[5] Two exceptions, neither of them (we believe) significant in the long run, occur to us. First, government may be pressured by a powerful industry simply to apply a subsidy and let price seek its own level (e.g., the "Brannan Plan" of unsavory memory in U.S. agriculture). Second, government

Electoral Systems and Balance of Consumer-Producer Power

Modeling the Stigler-Peltzman Support Function

The S-P iso-support curves appear to be little more than descriptions: a steeper curve simply says that politicians attend more to consumers whereas a flatter one says that pro- ducers' views matter more. To move beyond this description, we develop a simple model of political support, formalizing the S-P analysis. We then examine its comparative statics.

Assume that the regime is democratic, and that the incum- bent government, and the opposition, care about two things: (a) *legislative* (L), or parliamentary, support and (b) campaign funds, or, more generally, *money* (M).[6] Then, consistent with S-P analysis, we stylize political support S as a Cobb-Douglas function[7] of the form

$$S = M^{\alpha} L^{1-\alpha} \, | \alpha \in (0, 1) \tag{1}$$

may impose so-called sin taxes (e.g., on tobacco and alcohol) whose pro- fessed intent is to suppress consumption, thus moving (possibly) even above p_m.

[6] Alternatively, one could think of support purely in legislative terms, tak- ing legislative support as a function of votes and money (i.e., $S = L(V, M)$). So long as one acknowledged that the seats-votes elasticity was system- atically higher in majoritarian electoral systems, the result reported here would continue to obtain – and, indeed, could be demonstrated almost trivially. The form adopted here accepts that money can play an impor- tant role between, as well as during, elections, and therefore seems to us to conform better to experience.

[7] Only CES (constant elasticity of substitution) functions readily gener- ate the nicely tractable convex iso-support curves that the S-P approach assumes. Of CES functions, the Cobb-Douglas, where the constant elasticity is taken to be one, is the standard and simple workhorse; hence, we employ it here. It is also merely for notational convenience that we

Electoral Systems and Consumer Power

Legislative support – the share of seats in parliament, or, more broadly, the share of power that the government can command – is taken as an increasing function of vote share V, that is, $L = L(V)$, $dL/dV > 0$.[8] For simplicity we regard producers and consumers as mutually exclusive groups and assume – realistically, we believe – that consumers can contribute only votes whereas producers can offer both votes and money.[9] We assume, at least initially,[10] that consumers' support (in votes) will decrease in p (the price level), while producers' support (in both money and votes) will increase in π, the level of profits, as described earlier.

Formally, we have

$$M = M(\pi), \, dM/d\pi > 0 \tag{2}$$

and

$$V = V_p(\pi) + V_c(p), \quad dV_p/d\pi > 0, \quad dV_c/dp < 0, \tag{3}$$

take the exponents as summing to unity. As is well known from any standard textbook, the marginal rate of substitution – the quantity of theoretical interest here – is invariant to scale effects: see, e.g., Varian 1992, 98.

[8] In reality, electoral systems frequently violate even weak monotonicity, i.e., winning more votes may actually yield fewer parliamentary seats; the assumption of strong monotonicity is invoked here only to simplify modeling.

[9] Note that this assumption "stacks the deck" against our claim that electoral system matters for the shape of iso-support curves. If, by analogy to Denzau and Munger (1986, especially 93), we assumed that consumers could contribute only votes, producers only money, the greater steepness of majoritarian iso-support curves would follow almost self-evidently.

[10] We consider possible exceptions later, particularly in countries that depend heavily on exports in a few sectors.

where V_p denotes vote share from producers and V_c vote share from consumers.

With appropriate substitution from (2), (3), and the formula for L, we can rewrite (1) wholly in terms of π and p as

$$S = (M(\pi))^{\alpha} \left[L(V_p(\pi) + V_c(p)) \right]^{1-\alpha} ; \tag{4}$$

and from here we can determine the marginal rate of substitution (MRS)[11] between profits and prices, $d\pi/dp$, according to the conventional formula (or via the Implicit Function theorem)

$$\frac{d\pi}{dp} = -\frac{\partial S/\partial p}{\partial S/\partial \pi}. \tag{5}$$

Note first that

$$\partial S/\partial p = (M(\pi))^{\alpha}(1 - \alpha) L^{-\alpha}(dL/dV)(dV_c/dp) \tag{6}$$

while

$$\partial S/\partial \pi = \alpha(M(\pi))^{\alpha-1} (dM/d\pi) L^{1-\alpha}$$
$$+ (1 - \alpha)(M(\pi))^{\alpha} L^{-\alpha} (dL/dV) (dV_p/d\pi). \tag{7}$$

The MRS between profits and prices can then be stated as:

$$d\pi/dp = -\frac{dV_c/dp}{\dfrac{\alpha}{1-\alpha} \dfrac{\dfrac{M(\pi)}{dL/dV}}{L(V)} + \dfrac{dV_p}{d\pi}}. \tag{8}$$

---

[11] In terms of our graphical exposition, this is just the slope of the iso-support curve.

Because we can assume $dV_c/dp < 0$ while all other terms in (8) are positive, the MRS is *positive*, thus producing the upward-sloping S-P iso-support curves seen in Figure 2.1.

The comparative statics revealed by (8) accord with intuition for the most part. The iso-support curves become *steeper* (signifying greater consumer power and, all else being equal, lower prices) as:[12]

- Consumer votes become more responsive (or sensitive) to prices (dV_c/dp grows more negative);
- Politicians weight votes (as opposed to money) more heavily (decreasing α, hence increasing $1 - \alpha$); or
- Politicians already have more monetary support (higher M).[13]

Conversely, the curves become *flatter* – implying greater producer power and higher prices – when:

- Producers' votes or monetary contributions become more responsive to profits (rising $dM/d\pi$ or $dV_p/d\pi$)
- Politicians weight money more heavily (larger α), or

---

[12] Whatever decreases the denominator in (8) increases the *MRS*, i.e., implies steeper curves; whatever increases the denominator decreases the *MRS*, implying flatter iso-support curves.

[13] The two latter results suggest to us that either public funding of political parties and campaigns, or independently wealthy politicians, will tend to empower consumers and lower prices.

- The government already enjoys strong parliamentary support (L).[14]

Our most important result, however, was not at all intuitively obvious prior to this modeling exercise, but it is clear from (8): the iso-support curves become *steeper*, therefore, more consumer-friendly, as

- The seats-votes slope (dL/dV) – what we are calling here electoral responsiveness – increases.[15]

In other words, the greater the percentage increase in seats produced by a 1 percent increase in votes, the more policy will favor consumers and – assuming that the original S-P analysis is correct – the more closely prices will approximate the competitive price level p_c.

We focus the next stage of our analysis of democratic systems on the seats-votes ratio as a property of the electoral system, which determines variation in real prices between

[14] Thus, all else equal, countries with strongly dominant parties, whether of a nominally Leftist or Rightist persuasion, will disadvantage consumers. We argue that this is particularly the case in plurality SMD systems. And that indeed under extreme single-party dominance (what some used to call "one-and-one-half party systems"), PR actually advantages consumers more.

[15] Again: as dL/dV increases, holding all other terms constant, the overall denominator in (8) *decreases*; hence the *MRS increases*, implying a steeper iso-support curve.

democratic countries. Under normally competitive circumstances, majoritarian systems exhibit seats-votes slopes considerably higher – to be precise, one-and-one-half to eight times higher – than those of proportional systems. It follows directly that, if our model has accurately captured this aspect of reality, plurality systems – or those plurality systems in which leading parties divide the vote not too unequally – will be systematically more pro-consumer in their policies and will have significantly lower prices. Proportional representation (PR) systems, on the other hand, which by design do not greatly distort vote shares when converting them into seat shares, will be systematically more pro-producer in their policies and will have significantly higher prices.

To the best of our knowledge, this hypothesized link between seats-votes elasticity and pro-consumer policies went unobserved until the research of Rogowski and Kayser (2002). Yet it emerges clearly from our model, from the S-P approach more generally, and (we shall assert) from a careful examination of the empirical evidence. The intuition behind it may seem paradoxical to most students of politics: if one group can influence policy by both money and votes, another only by votes, then whatever increases the effect of the vote shifts policy toward the group that has *only* votes.[16] At a purely

[16] To forestall one possible misinterpretation of these results: it is *not* the case that producers would be better off if they gave no money, or if monetary contributions were outlawed: indeed, it is always the case that the

25

mechanical level, this is clear enough as one considers equations (5), (6), and (7) in tandem: any increase in dL/dV multiplies (6), the numerator of (5), by its full amount; yet, the same increase is diluted in (7), the denominator of (5), by the unchanged term in the first part of that sum, which represents the marginal effect of money.

Yet at a deeper level, this effect – that advantaging a given factor benefits disproportionately those who command *only* that factor – generalizes and seems less paradoxical. If, for example, one group in a society can offer only unskilled labor while another some mix of human capital and labor, we find nothing remarkable in the conclusion that an exogenous increase in the marginal productivity of unskilled labor will leave the unskilled better off.

Seats-Votes Slope: Quantifying Differences
Between Electoral Systems

Every electoral system may conveniently be regarded as a method for translating parties' or candidates' shares of the popular vote into shares of offices, typically of seats in parliament. Notationally, where V_i represents the ith party's

more sharply monetary contributions respond to increased profits, i.e., the higher the $dM/d\pi$ is, the more pro-producer policy will be (i.e., the flatter the iso-support curves).

($i \in [1,N]$) share of the popular vote and L_i its share of parliamentary seats (of course subject to the constraint $\sum V_i = \sum L_i = 1$), we characterize an electoral rule simply as a function r

$$L_i = r(V_i). \tag{9}$$

An important landmark of work on electoral systems was the observation by Taagepera and Shugart (1989) that virtually every extant electoral rule can be approximated[17] by a power function of the form

$$L_i = \frac{V_i^{\tau}}{\sum_{j=1}^{N} V_j^{\tau}}, \tag{10}$$

where V_i is the ith party's vote share, L_i is the same party's share of parliamentary seats, and N is the total number of parties.[18]

---

[17] The fit of actual data to the predicted curve is never perfect, but the essential insight – that more majoritarian systems are characterized by significantly higher seats-votes slopes in the competitive range – is extremely robust. That said, there are significant variations, owing to such factors as gerrymandering and geographical concentration of party support, in seats-votes slopes among majoritarian systems (and even among parties within majoritarian systems).

[18] King (1990) suggests the introduction of a bias parameter λ_i, such that Eq. 10 would be modified to

$$L_i = \frac{e^{\lambda_i} V_i^{\tau}}{\sum_{j=1}^{N} V_j^{\tau}};$$

and demonstrated how both parameters, "bias" and "responsiveness," could be estimated empirically.

Electoral Systems and Balance of Consumer-Producer Power

In systems of proportional representation, the exponent τ approximates one by design. In contrast, in plurality single-member district (SMD) systems – as used, for example, for elections to the British House of Commons or the U.S. House of Representatives – according to an observation current even in the early twentieth century (cf. Kendall and Stuart 1950), something like a cube rule prevails (i.e., $\tau \approx 3$). If, for example, four parties competed and won 10, 20, 30, and 40 percent of the vote, respectively, a typical plurality SMD system might award them (in the same order) 1, 8, 27, and 64 percent of the seats. In fact, as Taagepera and Shugart found, the typical plurality SMD system exhibits a value of τ closer to 2.5; while the U.S. Electoral College, because of its "winner-take-all" (bloc vote) provision in almost all states, has a historic value of approximately $\tau = 8$.[19] Subsequently, Richard Katz (1997, chap. 9, esp. table 9.11) estimated both parameters empirically, using King's (1990) procedure, for ninety-three countries and found that the twenty-six plurality SMD systems in his set had an average τ (in our terms) of 2.03 (with variance of about 1.6), while τ in forty-eight PR systems

---

[19] In reality, the magnitude of τ under plurality SMD in any particular country is mostly a measure of the country's political homogeneity. If each electoral district were a random draw from the entire voting population, every district would be marginal and τ would approach infinity; the more heterogeneous the districts, the greater the number of them that will be safe for one or another party – and, of course, the lower the value of τ. We discuss this point more fully later.

averaged 1.19 (with variance .13).[20] Bloc-vote systems (multi-member plurality), like the U.S. Electoral College, reached an average τ of 3.61 (with variance 5.4); but Katz's set included only seven such countries. Estimating the actual values of τ empirically proves exceedingly difficult, particularly in multi-party systems, but for the British Conservatives τ sometimes approaches 4.0.[21]

Economists and political scientists have long been interested, in other contexts, in the class of power functions represented by (10). Hirshleifer (1991), for example, following earlier work by Tullock, posited a "contest success function" of exactly this form, which related "fighting effort" to the probability of winning. He aptly designated the counterpart of τ as a "decisiveness" parameter (Hirshleifer 1991, 181). Even earlier, Theil (1969), from a purely normative standpoint and seemingly in ignorance of any empirical referent, suggested that seats *should* be allocated to parties by such a formula, and that the median voter's preference over the desirable value of τ should be decisive.

---

[20] In Katz's nine cases of *majority* SMD (with a run-off provision), τ averaged only 1.07 (variance: .21), i.e., less than under PR.

[21] An improved method of estimating responsiveness using district-level results from a single election (rather than pooling election results across elections) was introduced by Gelman and King (1994B); but it only applies to the case of two-party competition. More precise methods that generalize to the multiparty setting are introduced by Linzer (2009) and applied to the problem of estimating electoral "competitiveness" by Kayser and Linzer (2008).

A particularly revealing property of (10) is that, for the much simpler two-party case when each party captures half the vote ($V_i = .5$), τ expresses exactly the seats-votes elasticity, that is, the percentage increase in seats to be anticipated from a 1 percent increase in votes. Consider that in the two-party case,

$$L_i = \frac{V_i^{\tau}}{V_i^{\tau} + (1 - V_i)^{\tau}} = \frac{1}{1 + \left(\frac{1}{V_i} - 1\right)^{\tau}}$$

hence we have also

$$\frac{dL_i}{dV_i} = \frac{\tau \left(\frac{1}{V_i} - 1\right)^{\tau-1}}{\left(1 + \left(\frac{1}{V_i} - 1\right)^{\tau}\right)^2 V_i^2}$$

which self-evidently, for $V_i = \frac{1}{2}$, reduces to τ.

To put the matter concisely: in the two-party case under PR, moving from 50 to 51 percent of the popular vote raises a party's seat share by precisely the same margin; under plurality SMD, the same increase moves the seat share (give or take) to 52.5 percent; and in the U.S. Electoral College, such a division of the popular vote yields a candidate around 58 percent of the Electors (ignoring bias). The relationship between vote share (horizontal axis) and seat share (vertical axis) is plotted in Figure 2.2 for the three representative cases: PR ($\tau = 1$), plurality SMD ($\tau = 2.5$), and the Electoral College ($\tau = 8$).

The two-party scenario, with each capturing about half the vote, is highly relevant to non-PR systems because (a)

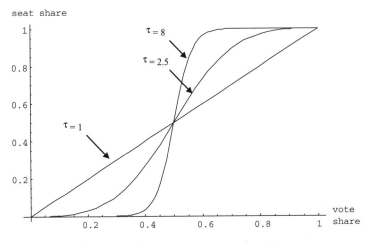

Figure 2.2. Two-party seat-vote functions

the higher the τ, the greater the disincentives to third-party formation (an effect commonly labeled Duverger's Law); and (b), under two-party competition on a single issue-dimension (Downs 1957), the dominant strategy for both parties is to converge on the position of the median voter and thus to win exactly half the electorate (cf. Persson and Tabellini 2000, ch. 3). Because in PR systems the seats-votes elasticity is normally $\tau = 1$, and because in plurality SMD systems under normally competitive circumstances (with each of two major parties capturing roughly half the vote) it will closely approximate τ, we can in most cases take τ in either system to be the seats-votes slope that we actually observe, or dL/dV.

Thus, for most purposes in this volume we will focus on the gross difference between SMD (or predominantly

SMD) and PR (or predominantly PR) systems, for two simple reasons: first, the real-world electoral systems we observe cluster around these two poles; and second, with very few exceptions, majoritarian systems have considerably higher seats-votes slopes than do proportional methods of election.[22]

The Effect of Competitiveness

An implicit assumption used earlier to contrast seats-votes slopes under various electoral systems is that the leading two parties divide the vote almost equally. This assumption is unnecessary for proportional systems – τ will equal one regardless of vote share – but is critical to plurality SMD. Precisely how great an effect a given vote swing has on seat share

---

[22] The United States, and even more some American states (e.g., California), have long been considered significant exceptions, because bipartisan gerrymanders, "vanishing marginals," or some combination of the two have made so many seats safe for incumbents, with effects we consider briefly in Chapter 5. Yet the 2006 congressional elections suggest the limits of this conventional analysis, and our seats-votes curves suggest why. In essence, "safe" seats simply flatten the curve around the midpoint – a uniform loss of 3 percent across all districts means only that the incumbent who normally wins by 60 percent now wins by only 57 percent – but make the curve all the steeper when the swing is big enough. A uniform loss of 10 percentage points across all districts means that suddenly *all* of the seats that the losing party had held by 60 percent are at risk.

under SMD systems depends on the closeness of political competition.

Our earlier example showed that where two parties evenly divide the vote in a two-party political system, a 1 percent increase in either party's vote share should translate into a 1, 2.5, and 8 percent increase in its respective seat share under proportionality, plurality SMD, and bloc vote electoral systems. However, what happens as the gap between the parties expands? For the simple two-party case, the shifting slopes along the SMD curve in the elementary seats-votes diagram suggest the answer.

The more imbalanced the two parties' vote shares become, the more the SMD slope decreases. In fact, when its slope drops below one, majoritarian electoral arrangements become less friendly to consumers than their proportional counterparts. Figure 2.3 reproduces the two-party seats-votes curve and adds vertical lines to indicate the points at which the SMD curve's slope equals one to delineate the area, A to B, in which majoritarian systems are more responsive to votes than PR. Figure 2.4 re-expresses vote shares as vote *margins*, the difference between the two parties' vote shares. Perhaps the most striking feature of both figures is the magnitude of the range over which SMD is more responsive than PR. As long as neither party gains more than roughly 40 percent more of the vote than its rival – a rare occurrence under two-party

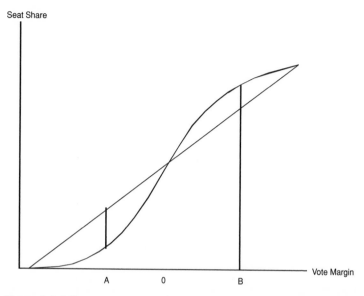

Figure 2.3. Where votes-seats slope becomes less under SMD than under PR

competition – SMD should be more consumer friendly than proportionality.

Precisely how does political competitiveness, measured as vote margin, affect the seats-votes relationship? Figure 2.4, as already noted, plots the marginal effect of vote share on seat share over a range of increasingly lopsided divisions of the vote. As we observed previously, SMD initially rewards more seats for a given shift in vote than proportionality. SMD begins with a seats-votes slope of 2.5 that diminishes remarkably slowly as long as politics remains reasonably competitive, remaining above two for vote margins above 15 percent and

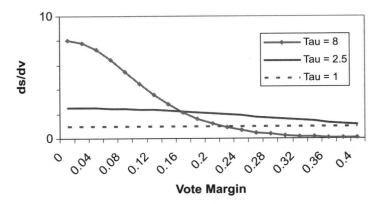

Figure 2.4. Competition and responsiveness

only dropping below that of PR ($\tau = 1$) after one party gains a vote share of forty percentage points greater than its opponent (i.e., in a two-party contest a margin of about 70–30).

The bloc vote system – again, the leading example is the U.S. Electoral College – drops off considerably faster than SMD, eventually offering a smaller marginal seat bonus than majoritarianism (at vote margins more than 16 percent) and PR (at vote margins more than 22 percent). Political competitiveness clearly matters for the effect of votes on seats.

Of course, it is not just party competitiveness that affects electoral systems' marginal seats-votes responsiveness but the converse as well: electoral systems influence the level of political party competition. The Downsian character of the two-party competition commonly found in SMD systems provides a strong incentive to competitive politics. The further a party deviates from the median voter under two-party competition along a single issue-dimension, the more disproportionate the share of the vote accruing to its more mainstream opponent. This nudges both parties to choose policies near the median and thereby keeps vote margins relatively small. The rare cases of protracted one-party dominance such as that enjoyed by the Revolutionary Institutional Party (PRI) in Mexico, the Congress Party in India, or the U.S. Democratic Party during the New Deal may provide the exception that tests the rule: policy should tilt sharply toward producers during such periods, and real prices should rise.

Of course, τ can vary among countries, and even among parties within a country, independent of any efforts by gerrymandering politicians to manipulate it; it is best regarded as an index of homogeneity of districts. To see this, imagine a country in which every electoral district is simply a random sample of the national electorate: for example, in the U.S. case, each House "district" would consist of a random draw of about 500,000 voters. Then, with the minor exceptions that the normal distribution would allow, each district would identically mirror the nation's overall political preferences – 51 percent of the vote nationally would mean 51 percent, give or take a few thousandths of a percentage point, in every district – and even an infinitesimal shift in national support would give the victorious party all of the parliamentary seats.

The fact that this does not happen in any known SMD parliament reflects the actual cultural and political heterogeneity of geographic districts: Oakland, CA, remains Democratic even when the nation votes 60 percent Republican, just as Nebraska votes Republican even in national Democratic landslides. Presumably the more heterogeneous the country, the lower its actual τ is under SMD; the more homogeneous – the more each district, in fact, approaches being a microcosm of the nation – the higher is its τ.

The notion of district as microcosm is not mere fantasy. As we discuss more fully later, a strong, directly elected national presidency, like that of France or most Latin American countries, in effect makes the whole country a single "district" and produces a τ approaching infinity.

Proportional electoral arrangements also have distinct effects on seats-votes responsiveness. Rather than converging toward the median, parties in multiparty PR systems can and often do stake out successful positions considerably removed from the median voter or along a different policy dimension. It is common to find small parties that represent narrow but stable segments of the population such as agriculture, specific ethnic groups, or small business. The volatility of given parties' vote shares between elections is likely to be considerably lower when voters choose parties based on ethnic, class, or religious loyalties rather than policy preferences. Moreover, large vote margins that would augur the demise of the second party in a two-party system (by permitting the entry of a rival) can comfortably persist in the absence of centripetal Downsian incentives.

Electoral arrangements also demand attention in our formal consideration of how vote competition affects responsiveness. To find the envelope of preferable electoral rules for consumer interests, we must consider not just how vote margins affect the seats-votes slope, dL/dV, but how this relationship changes under specific seat shares designated by those votes. The marginal response of seat share to vote share differs under various divisions of the legislature, which, in turn, are themselves a product of vote share and the electoral system. Thus, what we consider is $(dL/dV)/L(V)$, from the denominator of (8). If one plots $(dL/dV)/L(V)$ under our earlier specification as a function of V under PR ($\tau = 1$), plurality SMD ($\tau = 2.5$), and the Electoral College ($\tau = 8$), one gets the result shown in Figure 2.5.

Note that the "envelope" of highest lines is the most consumer-friendly position. For $V \leq .566$, this is the supermajoritarian Electoral College; for $V \in (.566, .684)$, it is plurality SMD; for $V \geq .684$, it is PR. PR is more pro-consumer than an Electoral College whenever $V > .59$.

The competitiveness of plurality systems depends, however, not only on the margin that separates the two leading parties but also on the volatility of voters' preferences. A party that wins 60 percent in one election, but knows from recent

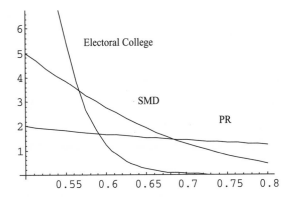

Figure 2.5. "Envelope" of most consumer-friendly systems at different levels of competitiveness in two-party systems

experience that it can easily sink to 40 percent when voters next go to the polls, is very different from one that confidently expects – perhaps because of deep religious, regional, or ethnic divisions – to win 60 percent at most elections. (Think of the nineteenth-century U.S. Republican hegemony, when Democrats could be dismissed as the party of "Rum, Romanism, and Rebellion"; or – as mentioned earlier – Northern Ireland under Unionist, i.e., Protestant, hegemony.)

For the general case, however, and returning to the model outlined earlier, we can substitute τ for dL/dV and rewrite (8) as

$$-\frac{dV_c/dp}{\dfrac{\alpha}{1-\alpha}\dfrac{\dfrac{M(\pi)}{\tau}}{L(V)}+\dfrac{dV_p}{d\pi}} \tag{8a}$$

39

and thus see the crucial theoretical prediction: normally, **the more majoritarian the system**, that is, the higher its τ,

- the steeper its S-P iso-support curves, and therefore
- the more pro-consumer its policies and
- **the lower its prices**, that is, the more closely they approximate p_c, the level that perfect competition would produce.

The most readily observable implication of the model is that about price levels; and we propose to test precisely that hypothesis, namely that **price levels will be systematically lower in majoritarian democracies**; and, indeed, that they will be lower **the more majoritarian the electoral system is**, that is, the **higher its τ**.

To return to an earlier point, a directly elected and powerful presidency, as is found in France or many Latin American democracies, has necessarily a τ that approaches infinity: winning the contest by even a single vote nationally confers all the power of the office (cf. King 1990, 162). As can be seen by inspection, such a high value of dL/dV would drive (10) also to infinity, implying an almost-vertical iso-support curve – and, of course, very low prices. Therefore, we shall also have to consider the separate effect of presidential systems in our empirical estimations.

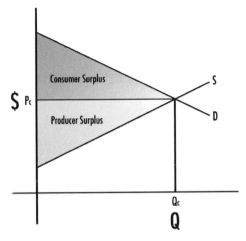

Figure 2.6. Welfare and distributional
effects at competition prices

Effects on Equality, Distribution, and Social Welfare

Let us stipulate that regulation can impede competition,
restrict supply, and impose higher prices. What further effects
does such regulation have, particularly on social welfare and
equality?

Begin with the most basic tool of Economics 1: the supply and demand curves depicted in Figure 2.6. In a competitive market, equilibrium price (P_c) and quantity supplied
(Q_c) are determined by the intersection of the supply and
demand curves; and the area below the price line but above
the supply curve describes producer surplus; the area above

41

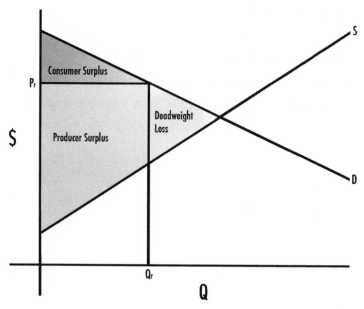

Figure 2.7. Welfare and distributional effects of pro-producer policies

the price line but below the demand curve represents consumer surplus.

If regulation restricts supply to Q_r (the "regulated" quantity), price will rise to P_r (Figure 2.7). Consumer surplus of course will shrink drastically, producer surplus may actually increase (particularly where consumer demand is most inelastic); and the infamous "deadweight loss" triangle, representing the quantity that willing purchasers now cannot buy and willing suppliers are prevented from offering, sums up the welfare that is forgone by the economy as a whole. Two points are clear even from this simple analysis: (a) restrictive policies unambiguously *diminish social welfare*; and (b) they also have powerful *distributional effects*, advantaging producers and disadvantaging consumers. Note that the more inelastic consumer demand is (i.e., the more steeply sloped is the demand curve), the stronger the distributional effects and the less the welfare effects.

Suppose we expand our picture of the economy to include two sectors, one labor- and one capital-intensive. Almost by definition, the labor-intensive sector is where the votes are, so in a democracy regulation will often favor producers in the labor-intensive sector. Under these conditions, the price of the labor-intensive product will rise relative to the capital-intensive one; and, if factors are mobile between the sectors, the familiar Stolper-Samuelson effect, illustrated in Figure 2.8, will obtain: the product's increased price will mean that less capital and labor are required to produce a dollar's worth of it, the iso-value curves in the labor-intensive sector shift to the southwest, and the line of relative factor prices grows steeper: wages rise relative to the rent of capital.[23] Because the wage-rent ratio is conventionally taken as an index of equality (see, e.g., O'Rourke and Williamson 1999), we can also say that supply-restricting policies in democratic regimes make

---

[23] As is also evident from the diagram, or from simple reflection, in both sectors capital will be substituted for some of the labor that has now become more expensive.

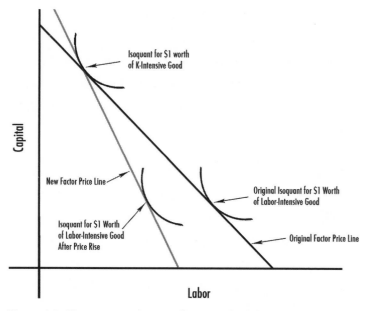

Figure 2.8. How pro-producer policies in the labor-intensive sector raise relative wages and diminish inequality

society more equal, albeit – as already seen – at the cost of an overall diminution of social welfare. However, as will be seen momentarily, this equalizing effect is conditional on labor remaining a mobile factor – and there are strong incentives to restrict that mobility.

In the conventional trade-related Stolper-Samuelson analysis, the gains to the abundant factor outweigh the losses to the scarce one because trade overall is welfare-improving. However, pro-producer policies inflict losses to the disadvantaged sector that outweigh the gains to the advantaged one.

Even so, we see analytically how the conventional observation can be correct: anticompetitive regulation in democratic settings normally leads to higher wages and greater equality.

To demonstrate empirical support for this seemingly counterintuitive notion that more regulation can lead to greater equality, we build on a recent contribution by Reuveny and Li (2003) that probes the effects of economic openness and democracy on income inequality. As a first cut, we construct a simple cross-national data set with the primary focus on the advanced democracies. Following their operationalization, the dependent variable is measured by a transformed Gini coefficient,[24] and we calculate the average over the 1970–2000 period. The independent variables, as specified in Reuveny and Li, are the level of democracy (i.e., polity score) and trade openness (i.e., exports plus imports over Gross Domestic Product [GDP]). Importantly, we expand Reuveny and Li's model by adding our key variable, the price level[25]; and, as we can see from Table 2.1, countries with higher price levels and – as we argue in this book, presumably greater regulation – are associated with less inequality of incomes.

Barriers to labor mobility, however, can reverse the equalizing effect. In Figure 2.9, the economy's entire labor supply is represented on the horizontal axis; workers to the left are

---

[24] That is, $\log(\frac{Gini}{1-Gini})$, with higher value indicating greater inequality.

[25] See subsequent chapters for a detailed discussion on this variable.

Table 2.1. The effects of regulation on income inequality

	Model 1
Price	−.004**
	[.001]
Democracy	.014
	[.032]
Trade openness	−.002***
	[.000]
Constant	−.220
	[.211]
Adjusted R^2	.447
N	20

Note: Robust standard errors are in brackets.
* $p < 0.1$, ** $p < 0.05$, *** $p < 0.01$. All tests are two-tailed.

employed in Sector A, workers to the right in Sector B. The line sloping downward from the left represents marginal productivity of labor (*MPL*, always of course decreasing in L) in Sector A, while the line sloping downward from the right describes (also declining) *MPL* in sector B. So long as labor is free to move between the two sectors, wages of course equalize at w_c; and at this point, Sector A employs workers to the left of vertical line L_c, Sector B, workers to the right of that line. Moreover, because summing the marginal products gives us the total product, we can take the area under the MPL_A curve to the left of L_c as the total product of Sector A; the area under the MPL_B curve to the right of L_c as the total product of Sector B. Distributional consequences are also clear from the graph:

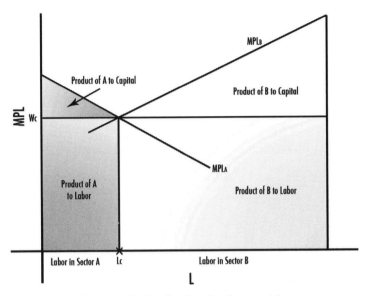

Figure 2.9. Welfare and distributional effects with a two-sector model with mobile labor

in each sector, the area of the lower rectangle, which is just the wage multiplied by the number of workers employed, is the share of total product in the given sector that goes to labor; the upper triangle, or the remainder of the total product of that sector, goes to capital.[26]

However, suppose that regulatory barriers prevent workers in B from moving into sector A. We can envision the barriers as analogous to the border of a state, and from standard migration models we know the result: if, as in Figure 2.10, only

---

[26] The figure assumes tacitly, as we do explicitly, that in the short run capital is sector-specific, i.e., does not move with labor.

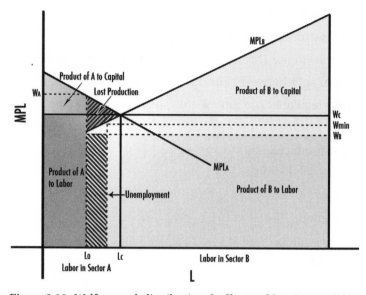

Figure 2.10. Welfare and distributional effects of barriers to labor mobility in a two-sector, two-factor economy

workers to the left of L_o, the "organized" allocation of labor, can be employed in A, then the wage in that sector is driven up to w_A, the wage in B falls to w_B, and the economy as a whole finds its welfare diminished by the area of the resultant "missing triangle." If a legal minimum wage, or a reservation wage enforced by norms or unions, prevents the wage in B from falling to w_B, we get unemployment (noted also in Figure 2.10) and a yet greater loss of social product.

Barriers to labor mobility also have distributional consequences: the wage-rental ratio rises (and thus inequality falls) in Sector A but declines (thus implying increased inequality) in Sector B.[27] Moreover, product per worker rises in the organized sector but falls in the unorganized one.

Thus, to use David Rueda's (2005, 2006) terms, when this kind of split between "insiders" and "outsiders" develops in highly regulated economies, the equalizing effect is confined to the privileged "insiders." Inequality grows between organized producers and the unorganized "outsiders" – with, of course, increasing welfare losses for the society as a whole. To the extent that international markets or technology-based innovation pushes down market wages, the gap between insiders and outsiders tends to grow, and we judge that this is already becoming the most serious challenge to the kind of highly regulated PR regimes that were established in many democracies in the period just before and just after World War II.

Exposure to International Markets

Our empirical work demonstrates what we would expect theoretically, namely that – controlling for all other effects,

---

[27] These results do not depend on the simplified straight-line graphics of the figures. In a Cobb-Douglas production function, for example, product per worker is $y = Y/L = A(K/L)^\alpha$, clearly decreasing in L (and hence increasing whenever L falls). Even more simply, the wage-rental ratio in this case is linear in the K/L ratio:

$$w/r = [(1 - \alpha)/\alpha](K/L), \text{ again clearly decreasing in } L.$$

including those of wealth, size, and electoral system – real prices decline as a country's exposure to international markets grows. Indeed, by definition in "small" countries, the price of traded goods and services is set in international markets. Only nontraded sectors, or traded ones protected by quotas or tariffs, could have domestic prices that exceeded "world" levels; and, where the home market is small, the deadweight costs of protection rapidly become prohibitive. So how do high-wage countries and sectors often do so well as exporters to world markets? Iversen and Soskice (2009) argue, and we agree, that such countries succeed chiefly by (a) large inputs of human capital that (b) are heavily subsidized (or, indeed, whose costs are totally borne) by these countries' governments. Assuming that this view is correct, as world prices of traded goods and services fall: (a) the domestic subsidies to human capital must increase and (b) the "wedge" between traded and nontraded sectors must widen.

What about Nondemocracies?

Given our emphasis on the marginal impact of votes on politicians' fates, one might expect dictatorships – in which, almost by definition, votes have no impact at all – to have the highest prices of all.[28] We disagree, regarding dictatorships as too

---

[28] We owe this argument to Federico Sturzenegger.

much of a mixed bag for us to have any coherent priors about their price levels. Some dictatorships indeed appear to be one-man (or one-couple) tyrannies on the Stalinist model: Ceauşescu's Romania and Saddam Hussein's Iraq come to mind. Others exhibit almost as much political contestation, albeit under different rules and with different "selectorates," as democracies. Some, vulnerable to city-dwellers' riots, create the kind of "urban bias" discussed by Lipton (1977) and Bates (1981), keeping foodstuffs and imports cheap. And still others, dominated by rural and export-oriented elites – for example, Brazil in the early twentieth century (Bates 1997, ch. 2) – keep both foodstuffs and imports dear. Without knowing whether and by whom a dictatorship is influenced, we cannot say *ex ante* whether it will strive to keep prices high or low – overall, or in particular sectors.

Are Electoral Systems Exogenous, and Does It Matter?

Suppose it is true that PR leads to more pro-producer policies, and that these policies lead to higher prices, more equality (at least in the "organized" sectors), and a greater loss of social welfare. Surely something in turn affects countries' choices of electoral systems (one friendly critic has suggested, only half in jest, that majoritarian systems are "only a proxy for speaking English"), and this of course raises the possibility of endogeneity and spurious correlation (both electoral system and policy are caused by something else, which we have failed to consider). In a provocative model with some supporting evidence, Ticchi and Vindigni (2010) propose that the median voter's choice of an electoral system will be constrained by the prevailing degree of economic inequality: more unequal countries choose majoritarian institutions, more equal ones PR.[29] Other scholars – Boix (1999), more recently Cusack, Iversen, and Soskice (2007) – have advanced more contingent historical arguments about the origins of PR in continental Europe.

The crucial test, we think, is this: does the electoral system have an independent and consistent effect on economic policy? We show in later chapters that it does. In other words, changing a country's electoral system affects prices in both the short and the longer run. Thus, while it is undoubtedly true – and later we tease out the argument – that other factors, including economic (in)equality, affect countries' choice of electoral systems, that choice itself has strong and predictable effects on economic policy.

In some ways, our argument on this point is analogous to the one many scholars now make about the link between Parliamentary Reform (expansion of the franchise) and repeal of the Corn Laws in the nineteenth-century United Kingdom.

---

[29] We advance a similar argument later in the chapter but show how this likely leads to self-sustaining equilibria of high or low inequality.

Electoral Systems and Consumer Power

While many factors – industrialization, urbanization, expanding world markets – pushed Britain toward more participatory rule (and, very likely, also toward freer trade), Parliamentary Reform gave a huge and likely crucial push toward the acceptance of free trade.

We turn now to the evidence: how do electoral systems affect policy and prices in democracies; is that effect uniform across rich and poor democracies; and in light of these facts, why do countries choose the electoral systems that they do?

3

Electoral Systems and Real Prices: Panel Evidence for the OECD Countries, 1970–2000

I n the article that originally motivated this book, Rogowski and Kayser (2002) performed only a plausibility check of the hypothesized link between electoral systems and real prices, based on cross-sectional analysis of OECD countries in 1990. The cross-sectional evidence was strongly support-ive, suggesting that real prices were, controlling for all other influences commonly adduced[1] and employing a broad array of robustness checks, about 10 percent lower in the average OECD country with single-member district (SMD) electoral systems than in those that used some form of proportional representation.

As with all new empirical claims – no one had previously even suggested a relationship between electoral arrange-ments and real prices – healthy skepticism was warranted. Indeed, recent research on related areas of public policy

---

[1] These include GDP per capita, trade openness, exchange-rate stickiness, and market size. Again, see the expanded explanation in a later footnote.

has contrasted with – but not contradicted – these price results, associating proportional electoral arrangements with such outcomes as (a) lower income inequality (Austin-Smith 2000; Birchfield and Crepaz 1998), (b) higher public spending (Persson and Tabellini 2003; Milesi-Feretti et al. 2002) or, in combination with central banking institutions, (c) greater price stability (Keefer and Stasavage 2003).[2] As we noted in the previous chapter, and will treat more extensively later

[2] Students of politics have analyzed and debated the effects – political, social, and economic – of electoral systems for almost a century and a half, beginning at the latest with a short passage in Walter Bagehot's classic work on *The English Constitution* (1867). Writing in 1941, Ferdinand A. Hermens blamed PR for the collapse of the German Weimar Republic, claiming that proportional electoral systems led inevitably to political polarization, policy paralysis, and the rise of anti-regime parties. Less controversially, Maurice Duverger propounded in the 1950s what he called "nearly...a true sociological law," namely "an almost complete correlation" between SMD and two-party systems – or, in the weaker form now known as "Duverger's law," that greater proportionality is associated with a higher number of parties. Douglas Rae (1971) categorized electoral systems and their effects, especially the effective number of parties and overrepresentation of large parties, laying down a path that all future work would follow.

More recent work has included, to name only a few of the most significant contributions, works by (in chronological order) Katz (1981, 1997), Powell (1982, 2000), Lijphart (1999), Roubini and Sachs (1989), Cox (1997), Birchfield and Crepaz (1998), Austen-Smith (2000), Persson and Tabellini (2003), and Cusack, Iversen, and Soskice (2007). From these and other sources, we now know with reasonable certainty that proportional methods of election are associated not only with more parties but with higher voter turnout; less strategic voting; less political violence; greater cabinet instability and shorter-lived governments; policy outcomes closer to the preferences of the median voter and, controlling for the position of the median voter, farther to the left; higher

Electoral Systems and Real Prices

(Chapter 7), these outcomes – some of them desirable on non-utilitarian (e.g., Rawlsian) normative grounds – are almost always purchased at the cost of an overall reduction in social welfare; but it remains a question of (social) taste whether more equal slices are preferred to a larger pie, or whether greater growth is worth greater volatility. In this chapter, we restrict ourselves to a closer study of the price relationship among OECD countries.

The original empirical analysis of Rogowski and Kayser (2002), though intriguing, left unaddressed questions of mechanism and dynamics in the relationship between electoral systems and real prices. Indeed, purely cross-sectional evidence cannot be conclusive on such substantively important issues. Despite the indirect corroboration of findings such as Scartascini (2002) that countries with majoritarian electoral systems have lower barriers to business entry, or Pagano and Volpin (2005), that proportional representation (PR) privileges entrepreneurs and employees over unorganized groups, a critical reader of the earlier paper might find the direct evidence wanting.[3] The relationship observed

governmental expenditures and budgetary deficits; more welfare and less "pork-barrel" spending; and greater equality of incomes.

[3] Relatedly, Hall, Iversen, Soskice, Estevez-Abe, and others (see, for a representative set of papers, Hall and Soskice 2001) have argued cogently that PR is the linchpin of an "organized market economy" characterized by anticompetitive mechanisms, and that these structures are so intermeshed with educational, labor-market, and political institutions as to be

between electoral systems and prices in Rogowski and Kayser (2002) could prove anomalous, spurious, or unfounded for too many reasons.

Most importantly, the observed effect might prevail only in 1990, the single year observed. The year 1990, for example, witnessed the beginning of a recession in a considerably larger proportion of majoritarian countries (including Australia, Canada, the United Kingdom, and the United States) than of proportional countries.[4] Depressed domestic demand could have diminished both components of real prices – nominal price baskets (PPP) and the exchange rate – yet, obviously, only a control for the latter could be included. Another anomalous event of 1990 was the first Gulf War. Might large military deployments have had distinct economic effects in those countries – all majoritarian: United States, United Kingdom, and France – that made the largest military commitments? Additionally, might the spike in oil prices from the anticipation and prosecution of the first Gulf War have raised prices less in OECD countries with domestic oil sources, which may have been disproportionately majoritarian (U.S., UK, Canada) rather than proportional (although Norway and

almost impervious to change. Lewis (2004) establishes the importance of competition and retail-sector efficiency for overall growth of productivity and income.

[4] See National Bureau for Economic Research (www.nber.org) and Economic Cycle Research Institute (www.businesscycle.com/pdfs/0012-businessChron.PDF).

the Netherlands would have been exceptions)? It is even possible that the Plaza Accord of 1985, which succeeded by 1990 in driving down the value of the dollar, may have affected prices differently in majoritarian than in proportional countries. Any one of these or many other possible anomalies would suffice to draw the reliability of conclusions founded on a 1990 cross-section into question.

Second, cross-sectional data cannot rule out a more enduring spurious relationship between electoral systems and real prices. Cross-nationally, countries with majoritarian and proportional systems exhibit systematic differences in many characteristics. Majoritarian electoral systems, for example, might simply be an instrument for British colonial heritage – an influence that, together with associated liberal market ideals, might explain both electoral arrangements and price levels. Panel data, such as those introduced here, permit fixed-effect models that absorb country-specific influences not articulated in the earlier specifications, and thereby assuage concerns about omitted variables. The implicit "natural experiments" of countries that switched electoral systems, but little else, during the panel period should similarly allay skepticism about such omitted variables. Moreover, use of fixed-effects models isolates the price effect, within countries, of a change in electoral system. Intertemporally, the use of panel data also enables us to explore the dynamic link between the price structure and its determinants (although we will deal with the intertemporal dimension more explicitly in Chapter 5). For instance, an increase in imports might lower prices through greater market competition, or a drop in unemployment might raise prices by stimulating consumption. None of these insights can be attained with cross-sectional data alone, nor can such data control for slow-changing or immutable national features. Panel data with country fixed-effects can exploit the natural experiments of electoral system change within countries while controlling for all cross-national effects.

A third problem arising from the systematic differences between countries of each electoral category is out-of-sample extrapolation. As Daniel Ho (2003) has noted, the price effect claims of the earlier paper often extended beyond what could be supported by the cross-sectional data. Because majoritarian countries differ so systematically from PR countries, inferences about the effect that majoritarian electoral arrangements have on prices extended beyond the available data range of the countries that used the other electoral system. Again, the panel data analyzed in this chapter at least partly remedy the problem: when countries change electoral systems, as do several in our panel sample, they provide overlapping variation to both electoral system categories. Juxtaposing the earlier Rogowski and Kayser findings with those of other authors noted earlier, more rigorous investigation promises considerable payoffs for our understanding of the role of electoral institutions in social spending, equality, and welfare.

Finally, and perhaps most saliently, Rogowski and Kayser were unable to preclude rival hypotheses. Characteristics of electoral systems other than seats-votes elasticities might affect regulatory incentives and barriers, and consequently real price levels. Consider two alternative mechanisms, untheorized and untested in Rogowski and Kayser (2002): differences in (a) campaign finance – state funding and limits on campaign spending may alter politicians' incentives and responsiveness to organized producers, and (b) clarity of governmental responsibility (cf. Powell 2000) – voters hold governments more responsible for changes in their real income and purchasing power when they are able to associate parties clearly with policies. Both of these rival explanations co-vary with the electoral system.

This chapter subjects the hypothesis of Rogowski and Kayser (2002) to more rigorous empirical scrutiny employing annual observations for twenty-three OECD countries over the period 1970–2000. This design permits country fixed-effects and enables the estimation of over-time effects of within-country changes in electoral systems: the shift from SMD to PR in France (1986) and New Zealand (1994); and from PR to SMD (or predominantly SMD) in France (1988), Italy (1993), and Japan (1994). Perhaps surprisingly, the results strongly support the original conjecture and indeed provide a better idea of how electoral-system change within a country affects consumer power and real prices. The panel analysis, after a variety of robustness checks, suggests that the long-term effect of a within-country change in electoral system is virtually identical (i.e., about a 10 percent change in prices) to that identified in the Rogowski-Kayser cross-sectional analysis as prevailing *between* countries with different electoral systems.

Why look first at panel data from the OECD countries, and not from the entire set of democracies around the world? Our reasons are chiefly two: (a) the underlying theory assumes that institutions and public policies have real effects, an assumption that may not hold in "weakly institutionalized" poorer democracies; and (b), the data for the OECD countries are simply better. To put the matter another way, we can say either: (a) the present OECD panel study serves as a considerably expanded plausibility check (if our hypothesis does not hold here, it would likely hold nowhere); or (b) our later investigation of worldwide data (Chapter 4) is a robustness check, on which in fact we had considerably lower expectations that the hypothesis would hold among poorer democracies.

Our underlying theoretical model has been presented in Chapter 2. We simply emphasize here its chief implication, which should hold cross-sectionally and intertemporally among well-institutionalized democracies, that is, controlling for other factors, countries with majoritarian electoral systems will have lower prices; and countries that change from PR to majoritarian electoral systems will decrease their average price levels.

It is instructive at this point to observe that, in the real world, governments manifestly do inhibit competition, and keep prices high, through an astonishingly inventive variety of measures; and that practicing politicians and policy advocates frequently note, or even more frequently simply take for granted, that PR regimes favor the enactment and survival of such measures.

In relatively open economies,[5] competition-inhibiting measures naturally concentrate on *nontraded* goods and services, and on the nontraded component of otherwise tradable goods (e.g., the retail price of apparel): construction, retailing of all sorts, baking, barbering, banking, printing, insurance, teaching, lawyering, hotel keeping, and medical and pharmaceutical services (to name only a few) may easily be restricted as to (*inter alia*) licensure, hours and size of operation, discounting, advertising, and compulsory guild, union, or associational membership.[6] Overall, such a system will (as intended) keep prices high, and indeed will impose further costs not fully captured by prices: the opportunity costs of

---

[5] We find consistently that openness itself – measured as the import share in GDP and controlling for population size – powerfully restrains prices.

[6] For convincing real-world examples, see Lewis (2004) and Walker (2004).

extra search and shopping, the dynamic costs of weak innovation, the incentives to prefer leisure over labor.

Against its obvious disadvantages must be set the (equally, or to some more) obvious advantages of such a system: higher wages, less inequality, greater security of employment, greater leisure, greater variety (particularly of services), more expert service, higher-quality goods, even perhaps a "de-commodification" of work (Esping-Andersen 1990). We have addressed briefly, and will consider further in a concluding chapter, the classical welfare losses that follow directly from restricting competition, but we do not intend to neglect the advantages of such a system that we enumerate here. The normative assessment of which basket of outcomes is superior must, as noted earlier, ultimately be left to the preferences of the citizens affected.

In any event, it is precisely where voters are empowered that such market competition should be least fettered. Consider the incentives of both legislators and voters under the mechanism we posit. Legislators respond to both money and votes in optimizing their probability of retaining office. Barring systematic differences in campaign finance across electoral systems – a rival hypothesis that we test and reject – systems that magnify the effect of even small swings in the vote on the incumbent party's seat share should tilt the balance of legislators' (and their regulatory agents') attention in favor of consumers. Although organized producers – among them union members – also contribute votes, any institutional arrangement that increases the effect of a single factor will increase the influence of the group that provides only that factor. Voters, for their part, are perceived by legislators as responding, and likely do respond, to the improved purchasing power provided by a reduction in real prices by rewarding incumbents.[7] A majoritarian electoral system is thus likelier, at the margin, to produce pro-consumer, low-price policies, while a proportional system is likelier, also at the margin, to enact pro-producer, high-price policies.

Increasingly, politicians, policy experts, and advocates and opponents of economic reforms perceive this same link. In Germany's efforts to reform its exceptionally troubled system of local monopolies (e.g., in bakeries), cross-ownership of shares, highly restrictive retail hours, and labor-market rigidities, advocates of change have come increasingly to see the PR electoral system as a major obstacle (Quitzau 2002, 5). In Italy, as we demonstrate at greater length in a later chapter, advocates of economic reform saw a majoritarian electoral system as the *sine qua non* of a more competitive policy; and in New Zealand, the radical economic reforms of the 1980s were

---

[7] Indeed, the success of increasingly precise measures of voter welfare such as real disposable income – i.e., income adjusted for inflation and net of taxes – in predicting election outcomes (cf. Bartels and Zaller 2001) suggests that politicians may be correct in assigning great weight to the material welfare of their constituents.

made possible by an SMD system and – again, in the view of advocates of reform – have been halted or actually reversed by the switch to a PR system (Alvey 2000).

As a necessary prologue to the data analysis, we next consider issues of measurement and of model specification.

I. How to Measure and Compare Price Levels Cross-Nationally and Over Time

The standard method in the literature for comparing price levels cross-nationally is known as "purchasing power parity over exchange rate,"[8] or for short PPP/XR. It can readily be made transparent: Suppose that some standard good or service – let us say, for simplicity, a man's shirt of a particular brand and size – costs $50 in the United States but that the identical shirt is marketed for €100 in France. Suppose also that on exchange markets the dollar trades at parity with the Euro. Then a French consumer or merchant could convert the €100 into $100, go to (or order from) the United States, and get two shirts for the same money that would have bought him only one in France. In this sense, the price of the shirt is exactly twice in France what it is in the United States. In terms

---

[8] This is simply the inverse of the so-called "real exchange rate," i.e., XR/PPP.

of purchasing power, because PPP/XR = 2/1, French prices are twice those of the United States.

The standard efforts to compare prices cross-nationally, including particularly the International Comparisons Project (ICP) that produces the Penn World Tables, simply broaden this exercise to compare PPP/XR with respect to broad "baskets" of goods and services, of the kind that are familiar from calculations of consumer price indices. If the broadest possible "basket," representing all of the goods and services that a typical economy might consume, costs (let us say) €5,000 in Italy but $3,000 in the United States, while the Euro-dollar exchange rate is 1:1, then we can say that the overall price level in Italy is 5/3, or 1.6 times, what it is in the United States.[9]

In theory, any substantial cross-national price differences should be quickly arbitraged away. For this reason, theory suggests that real prices for identical goods should be the same everywhere: this is the well-known Law of One Price (LOP). In practice, as a considerable literature shows, the LOP obtains only in highly attenuated form (see, *inter alia*, Kravis and Lipsey 1988; Clague 1986; Bergstrand 1991). Several factors have long been understood, empirically if not theoretically, to make for persistent differences in price levels.

---

[9] In practice, international price level comparisons adjust national baskets to account for local tastes, e.g., substituting beer in the German "basket" for wine in the French one. The International Comparisons Project has done this with considerable care and sophistication.

Foremost among these is **wealth**, usually measured as real GDP per capita. Richer countries, independent of other plausible factors, have higher real prices, a result that is robust across virtually every possible specification. Wealth, indeed, consistently emerges as the most important single determinant of national price levels, even when one controls for the two most commonly imputed causes (Bergstrand 1991), namely (a) differences in productivity between traded and nontraded sectors (Belassa 1964; Samuelson 1964) and (b) cross-national differences in capital/labor ratios (Kravis and Lipsey 1983; Bhagwati 1984).[10]

Second, there are obvious **natural, cultural, and policy barriers** to arbitrage. Our general prior here is that economies that are less open – whether because of physical isolation, idiosyncratic or xenophobic tastes, or their governments' isolationist tendencies – will be better able to maintain prices above world levels. Our overall measure is simply imports as a share of GDP,[11] and we anticipate that – again, all else equal – greater openness entails lower prices.

---

[10] Wealthier consumers may also be less price sensitive, allowing for pricing-to-market (Krugman 1987).

[11] We are well aware of the possible shortcomings of this summary measure, but (a) it is the one most readily available for our whole panel, (b) we have ascertained in cross-sectional analyses that it correlates at .9 or better with such more sophisticated measures of openness as deviations from a gravity model (see, e.g., Lee 1993), and (c) our insertion of a control for population size (see text) in any event gives us something more akin to a gravity model.

Third, we conjecture that **market size**, proxied here simply by the country's population, will be inversely related to price because of (a) the specialization a large domestic market permits[12] and (b) simple economies of scale. Moreover, because trade (or import) share of GDP is known to be inversely related to population size – small countries, all else equal, trade more – inserting this control for "natural" openness makes our imports/GDP variable a better test of the effects of "policy" openness.

Fourth, as changes in demand can affect both components of real prices (nominal prices and the exchange rate), we control for business cycles by including GDP growth. Our priors here are less obvious because, by also controlling for exchange rate fluctuations (see later), we are effectively simulating a "gold standard" of irrevocably fixed exchange rates. Just as economic expansion lowered price levels during the nineteenth-century gold standard, so should it here: imagine, for example, that a country doubles cheese production but that the money supply and exchange rate remain fixed; where a dollar used to buy two units of cheese, it is now equivalent to four. Thus economic growth, all else equal, lowers real prices.

Finally, and crucially in any time-series analysis, we must control for (a) exchange-rate fluctuations and (b), because of

---

[12] As Adam Smith (*Wealth of Nations*, I:3) first noted, "The Division of Labour is Limited by the Extent of the Market"; hence, in many specializations price will decrease as market size increases.

indexation issues, the U.S. rate of inflation. We discuss each separately.[13]

(a) **Sharp changes in a country's exchange rate:** That domestic prices remain "sticky" even under significant changes in a country's exchange rate is a commonplace of the literature, and indeed the whole reason that currency devaluations help to remedy imbalances on the current account; but this will have obvious and significant effects on the price level as defined by PPP/XR. Suppose the Argentine peso (to take a not-so-distant example) previously traded at parity with the U.S. dollar but suddenly devalues to a peso-dollar exchange rate of 4:1. Although we do not expect that all Argentine prices (in peso terms) immediately quadruple, they will certainly rise. [14] Suppose that Argentine prices only double in terms of PPP (i.e., the peso price of a given

---

[13] One might naturally suspect that some of the variance in real price levels results from differences in factor endowments, including physical capital, human capital (often proxied by education levels), and even arable land or other natural resources. In practice, however, capital/labor ratios and education measures are too highly correlated with wealth (measured by GDP per capita) to permit analysis of their separate effect on prices, if any; and per capita endowment of arable land is consistently insignificant. We therefore omit any measures of factor endowments in the present tests.

[14] Indeed, if PPP moved in perfect tandem with exchange rate, devaluations would have no point.

basket of goods doubles). Then the devaluation has effectively halved real Argentine prices: if previously PPP/XR equaled p, then the new price level would be $2p/4$ or exactly half what it previously was. We therefore employ year-to-year change in the given country's exchange rate – that is, the percentage increase or decrease from the previous year's nominal exchange rate against the U.S. dollar, $(XR_t - XR_{t-1})/XR_{t-1}$ as a control variable throughout our panel estimations.[15] Obviously, when XR rises but PPP is sticky, we expect real prices to decline; hence, the sign on this coefficient should be negative. In other words, we anticipate that a currency *depreciation* will be associated with *lower* real prices, while an *appreciation* will lead (at least in the short run) to higher real prices.

(b) If it is chiefly the United States that is undergoing an exchange-rate fluctuation, the problem is amplified because conventional measures of real prices (on which we also rely) are anchored to U.S. prices. Suppose the dollar is appreciating against all other currencies (as it did in the late 1980s): then XR for all

---

[15] For present purposes, we thus take nominal exchange-rate variation as exogenous. In fact, of course, it is very much an object of government policy; and we take it as a topic for future research to consider whether particular political institutions are biased toward particular exchange-rate policies.

other countries will rise (a dollar will buy more units of the local currency), and real prices (PPP/XR) outside the United States will fall. Conversely, if the dollar falls against other currencies – as it did under the chronic U.S. budgetary and current account deficits of the George Bush years – real prices outside the United States should rise. What we need is a "floating anchor" that takes into account internally driven changes[16] in the specific value of the U.S. currency, and we therefore insert the U.S. inflation rate (GDP deflator) as a control variable. When the United States is undergoing (or is anticipated to undergo) high inflation, the dollar will (according to standard currency-rate theory) depreciate against other currencies, leading every other country's XR – the units of its currency that a dollar will buy – to fall; when the dollar's domestic purchasing power is stable, it often appreciates against other currencies, leading the other countries' XR to rise. The expected sign on the coefficient of U.S. inflation should therefore be positive.

The measurement, data source, and summary statistics of all of the variables are presented in the Appendix.

---

[16] An obvious alternative measure, the U.S. deficit on current account, would often be driven by external factors, e.g., foreigners' willingness to invest in the United States.

II. The Panel Data and Empirical Testing

1. The Data

We analyze annual price data (PPP/XR) for twenty-three OECD countries[17] between 1970 and 2000. The price level for a given country in any year is indexed to U.S. prices so that (e.g.) a figure of 106 – as it happens, the mean over the whole period for this set of countries – signifies that overall prices are 1.06 times U.S. levels.

The dependent variable, purchasing power parity over exchange rate (PPP/XP), has a mean, as just mentioned, of around 106, a standard deviation of 24.6, and a range of 39.9 to 187.1. Preliminary analysis shows a large cross-country variation and – witness Figure 3.1 – generally higher real price levels in PR than in SMD systems.

2. Empirical Analysis

We first establish whether our dependent variable is stationary. As is well known, when the dependent variable is not

---

[17] The set consists of all twenty-four states that were members of the OECD in 1990, except Turkey, for which data are inadequate. The countries included are thus Australia, Austria, Belgium, Canada, Denmark, Finland, France, Germany, Greece, Iceland, Ireland, Italy, Japan, Luxembourg, the Netherlands, Norway, New Zealand, Portugal, Spain, Sweden, Switzerland, the United Kingdom, and the United States. Note that the periods under dictatorship in Greece (until 1974), Portugal (until 1975), and Spain (until 1977) are excluded.

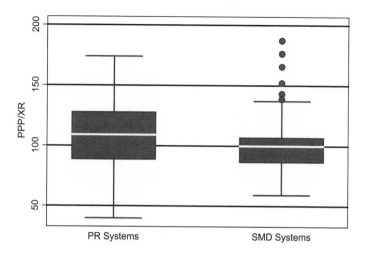

Figure 3.1. Purchasing power parity over exchange rate by electoral systems

stationary, the underlying data-generating process does not remain constant over time; hence the usual t-statistics will have nonstandard distributions and will generate misleading inferences. Our preliminary visual examination of the dependent variable, as plotted in Figure 3.2, finds no discernible trend (except in the case of Japan), and we conjecture that our dependent variable is stationary. To test in a more systematic way whether unit roots are present, we implement the Levin-Lin test in our cross-sectional time series data. The results, as shown in the upper panel of Table 3.1, indicate no evidence of nonstationarity. Because it is sometimes asserted that the Levin-Lin test (and other tests for unit roots in general) enjoys

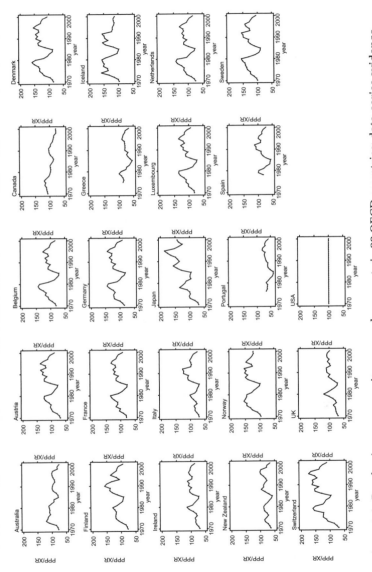

Figure 3.2. Purchasing power parity over exchange rate in 23 OECD countries: data-series evidence No consistent, discernible trend, suggesting that the dependent variable, real price levels, is stationary.

Table 3.1. Estimation results of panel unit roots tests

PPP/XR: Levels				
Levin and Lin tests	**Coefficient**	**_t_-value**	**_t_***	**_p_**
Constant	−0.2718	−10.602	−4.2652	<0.0001***
Constant, trend	−0.3677	−12.348	−3.2171	0.0006***
Im, Pesaran, & Shin tests	**_t_-tar**	**CV1%**	**Ψ**	**P**
De-meaned, no trend	−2.355	−1.980	−4.168	<0.001***
De-meaned, trend	−2.699	−2.590	−2.815	0.002***

Notes:
Levin and Lin tests augmented by 1 lag. H_0: nonstationarity
coefficient: Coefficient on lagged levels.
t-value: t-value of coefficient.
t*: transformed t-value. $t* \sim N(0, 1)$
p: p-value of t*; ***: $p < 0.01$.
Im, Pesaran, & Shin tests augmented by 1 lag. H_0: nonstationarity
t-bar: mean of country-specific Dickey-Fuller tests.
CV1%: 1 % critical value of the Im, Pesaran, and Shin tests
Ψ: transformed t-bar statistics. $\Psi \sim N(0, 1)$.
p: p-value of Ψ; ***: $p < 0.01$.

only limited explanatory power, we double-check for nonstationarity by using the Im-Pesaran-Shin test. The results from the lower panel of Table 3.1 suggest again that our dependent variable is stationary. Therefore, we proceed assuming stationarity of the dependent variable.

Model 1, incorporating all of the control variables discussed earlier into the model specification, tests the price-reducing effect of SMD systems. During our model-building process, we first are concerned with the possibility that the spherical errors assumption might not hold in our data set. Belgium and Luxembourg, to take a minor but clear example, were in a full currency union throughout this period and hence are not independent observations on the exchange-rate variable. We regard this as an empirical question, and the empirical results from the Breusch-Pagan LM test of independence and the modified Wald test for group-wise heteroskedasticity indicate strongly that the errors are not spherical. Accordingly, we reestimate the model by using panel-corrected standard errors, as originally proposed by Beck and Katz (1995), to guard against potential problems of panel heteroskedasticity across countries and contemporaneous correlation of error. Note that we also include the lagged dependent variable to account – albeit imperfectly, as we shall see – for first-order autocorrelation.

The result, confirming the visual impression of Figure 3.1, suggests strong negative price-level effects of SMD systems. According to this model, a short-run shift from PR systems to SMD systems leads to a reduction of price levels by 1.2 units (recall that the baseline is 100 in the United States). In the average OECD country, with a price level of 105.88, this amounts to a 1.1 percent drop in prices. In the long run, the "market basket" of goods and services under SMD systems is cheaper than under PR in the average OECD country by

11 percent,[18] and half of the long-term change will be achieved in 6.6 years.[19] We note also, here and in the subsequent models, that the estimated coefficients on our control variables are consistently of the expected sign, albeit not in every case statistically significant.

As Kittel and Winner (2005) note, cross-sectional time-series analysis may be unreliable owing to its sensitivity to the inclusion of country and year dummies. This pooled specification, of course, runs the risk of omitted-variable bias, most notably from such unobserved country-specific characteristics as political culture, geography, or institutional inheritance (e.g., a common-law system). To guard against this possibility, Model 2 of Table 3.2 reestimates the model with country fixed-effects: the country dummy variables now pick up any country-specific intercept that is not accounted for elsewhere. Model 3 in turn explores annual fixed-effects. By including year dummies, we would be able to eliminate any bias caused by unaccounted trends and external shocks to which all these OECD countries might have been jointly exposed. Importantly, as we can see from Model 2 and Model 3, our substantive finding – that SMD reduces price – is insensitive to the inclusion of both country and year effect. Yet, upon

---

[18] $((1.198/(1 - .9000))/105.6 = .1134.$
[19] $- \log 2/\log (.9) = 6.58$ years.

Electoral Systems and Real Prices

Table 3.2. Model results: Dependent variable is purchasing power parity over exchange rate, PPP/XR

	Model 1 PPP/XR Pool	Model 2 PPP/XR FE(Country)	Model 3 PPP/XR FE(Year)	Model 4 PPP/XR FE(Decade)
Lagged Dependent Variable	.900*** [.022]	.842*** [.030]	.886*** [.021]	.863*** [.022]
Single-member district	−1.198*** [.461]	−2.317*** [.830]	−1.684*** [.589]	−1.727*** [.493]
Real per capita GDP	.0001 [.0001]	.0003*** [.0001]	.0003*** [.0000]	0.0003*** [0.0001]
Imports as a share of GDP	−0.128*** [0.020]	−0.048 [.049]	−.103*** [.015]	−.126*** [.017]
Population, log	−2.021*** [0.343]	−36.179*** [7.333]	−1.429*** [.247]	−1.837*** [.313]
GDP growth rate	.051 [.135]	−.193 [.124]	−.002 [.115]	−.090 [.129]
Change in exchange rate	−0.735*** [0.040]	−.759*** [.038]	−.518*** [.049]	−.672*** [.041]
U.S. Inflation rate	0.300* [0.165]	.406*** [.151]	dropped	−0.026 [.189]
Constant	47.088*** [6.729]			
Joint significance of fixed effects		.000***	.000***	.000***
N	666	666	666	666

Note: Panel-corrected standard errors in brackets. * $p < 0.1$, ** $p < 0.05$, *** $p < 0.01$. All tests are two-tailed. The individual country coefficients (including the constant) in fixed-effects models are omitted in the interest of space.

further consideration, two theoretical reasons impel us not to put much stock in annual fixed-effects.

First, our previous control variable, the U.S. inflation rate, provides a more coherent theoretical linkage between the common external shocks and the dependent variable than does a set of annual dummies. Secondly, the notion of annual fixed-effects is deceiving in the sense that the number of years in the model is theoretically unbounded as time goes to infinity. Econometrically, Neyman and Scott (1948) show that one's estimates can be inconsistent if the model includes variables that increase in tandem with the number of observations (aka, "the incidental parameter" problem). Therefore, instead of using year dummy variables, we include *decade* dummy variables to capture the time dimension in Model 4. From Model 4, we can clearly see that SMD electoral systems continue to show significant and strong negative price effects. We observe also that the coefficient of *USAINF* loses its significance once we include the year or decade fixed-effects – exactly as one might expect, because the variable USAINF is unit-invariant and highly correlated with the time dummies.[20]

---

[20] Parenthetically, we note also that the coefficients on the decadal dummies (using the 1970s as the baseline) are negative, suggesting the possibility that real prices relative to the United States were consistently dropping over this period. We also integrate country fixed-effects and decade fixed-effects in a unifying model, and our empirical results are again sustained.

3. Robustness Checks

To buttress our empirical analysis further, we now undertake a series of robustness checks. Particularly, we pay special attention to several substantive and methodological issues that are related to the construction of the dependent variable, the independent variables, and the model specification.

First, one might reasonably suspect that different electoral systems are associated with respectively different levels of taxation that, in turn, yield the price differences that we have attributed to differences in competition policy and regulation. Indeed, a comparison of consumption tax levels (value added and sales tax) shows consumption taxes to be higher in proportional systems, as Beramendi and Rueda (2007) have convincingly shown (cf. Chapter 7, later). Nevertheless, Model 5 in Table 3.3 uses prices *net of tax*[21] as a new dependent variable instead of PPP/XR. The SMD coefficient remains negative, significant, and nearly of the same magnitude as with the unmodified dependent variable. Consumption taxes may be higher in PR systems (1) because value-added tax (VAT) is preferred over sales tax in most PR countries and (2) because VAT levels are usually higher than sales taxes; but as Lindert (2003)

---

[21] Calculated using mean VAT or sales tax rate across all categories of goods and services. Source: OECD Revenue Statistics, www.sourceoecd. org. Note that we use the mean VAT and sales tax rates across all goods and services as opposed to standard rates, which are subject to many exemptions or reductions for many sectors.

Table 3.3. Robustness checks

	Model 5: Net of Tax FE(Decade)	Model 6: PPP/XR Pool	Model 7 PPP/XR GMM	Model 8 PPP/XR Pool
Lagged Dependent	.836***	.900***	.801	.903***
Variable	[.023]	[.022]	[.040]	[.017]
Single-member district	−1.822***		−4.407**	−.976*
	[.424]		[2.103]	[.510]
SMD plurality system		−1.188*		
		[.623]		
SMD majority system		−1.173**		
		[.461]		
Reinforced PR system		.207		
		[.525]		
Campaign regulation				1.069***
				[.251]
Clarity of responsibility				−.161
				[.291]
Real per capita GDP	0.0004***	.0001	.0008***	.0001
	[0.0001]	[.0001]	[.0002]	[.0001]
Imports as a share of GDP	−.100***	−.127***	.146	−.080***
	[.017]	[.020]	[.094]	[.017]
Population, log	−1.185***	−2.029***	−21.858	−.904***
	[.314]	[.346]	[27.485]	[.156]
GDP growth rate	−.226**	.049	−.319***	−.034
	[.110]	[.137]	[.086]	[.092]
Change in exchange rate	−.654***	−.736***	−.721***	−.956***
	[.038]	[.137]	[.107]	[.027]
U.S. Inflation rate	−.006	.302*	.237*	.235*
	[.177]	[.168]	[.136]	[.123]

Electoral Systems and Real Prices

	Model 5: Net of Tax FE(Decade)	Model 6: PPP/XR Pool	Model 7 PPP/XR GMM	Model 8 PPP/XR Pool
Constant		47.134***	−.724***	25.847***
		[6.747]	[.179]	[3.393]
Joint significance of fixed effects	.000***			
N	656	666	642	666

Note: Panel-corrected standard errors in bracket except in Model 7 where robust standard errors are reported.
* p < 0.1, ** p < 0.05, *** p < 0.01. All tests are two-tailed. The decade coefficients (including the constant) in Model 5 are omitted in the interest of space.

suggests, the causality is most likely the reverse: PR countries prefer a generous welfare state that demands higher taxes. PR countries therefore choose the most efficient consumption tax system (VAT) to minimize the distortions of their relatively high tax levels. In short, consumption taxes and prices net of tax show the same, theoretically consistent, result: both are substantively and statistically higher in PR systems.

Second, one might object that our key explanatory variable, SMD, is too crude to capture the notion of seats-votes elasticity, or "responsiveness" (see King 1990; Katz 1997, esp. chap. 9). Alternatively, others might question whether our empirical model is inadequate to entertain the heterogeneity across countries. To address these issues, we first refine our measurement by expanding our electoral system variable into four categories presumably in descending order of seats-votes elasticity:[22] (1) SMD plurality (U.S., UK, Canada, and New Zealand before 1994, plus "mixed" but predominantly SMD plurality systems (Italy and Japan after 1993); (2) SMD majority (Australia, France except 1986–1988); (3) "reinforced" PR[23] (Japan before 1993, Greece, Spain) plus Single Transferable Vote (STV; Ireland); and (4) pure or nearly pure PR (Austria, Belgium, Denmark, Finland, Germany, Iceland, Italy before 1993, Luxembourg, Netherlands, New Zealand since 1994, Norway, Portugal, Sweden, Switzerland). Our expectation, of course, is that these four categories will also affect prices in descending order (SMD-plurality will lower them most, pure PR least). To test this hypothesis, we create dummy variables for each category, leaving pure PR as the baseline for comparison. Then, we replace the SMD dummy with these three finer-grained variables and refit the model. As shown in Model 6, the effects do follow a descending order of magnitude. However, neither the difference between SMD plurality and SMD majority systems, nor the difference between "reinforced" and "pure" PR, is statistically significant. Therefore,

---

[22] We have also considered such more traditional measures of system proportionality as district magnitude, effective number of parties, and effective threshold; but these, it seems to us, do not accurately reflect seats-votes elasticity. For a specific examination of the effect of district magnitude, see Rogowski and Kayser (2002).

[23] The "reinforced" systems award the largest party a considerably higher share of seats than of votes.

we stick to our original parsimonious categorization and continue to use the SMD variable to capture the effect of electoral systems.

To further account for the unobserved heterogeneity across countries, we next consider a dynamic panel model in which we introduce unobservable unit heterogeneity into the error term.[24] Under such a circumstance, the lagged dependent variable model (as used from Model 1 to Model 6) will yield biased and inconsistent estimation due to the correlation between the lagged dependent variable and the composite error term. The bias remains of order $1/T$ even if we attempt to remove the unobserved heterogeneity by using the fixed effect estimator (Baltagi 2001). Hence, we turn to the Arellano–Bond generalized method of moments estimator (GMM) (Arellano and Bond 1991).[25] The results, presented in Model 7, continue to support a strong price-reducing effect of SMD systems even after we explicitly model the unobservable heterogeneity across countries.

---

[24] Formally, our dynamic panel data structure takes the form of $y_{i,t} = \sum_{i=1}^{j} p y_{i,t-j} + X_{i,t} B + \varepsilon_{i,t}$, where $\varepsilon_{i,t} = \alpha_i + u_{i,t}$.

[25] Briefly summarized, the idea of this GMM estimator is to use first-differencing transformation to remove the unobservable unit effect. The resultant correlation between $\Delta y_{i,t-1}$ and $\Delta u_{i,t-1}$ from the transformation procedure is then instrumented out by using the dependent variable and all independent variables from two lags and before. For a detailed discussion of dynamic panel data in political science, see Wawro (2002).

Table 3.4. Jackknife analysis

	Maximum coefficient	Country omitted at max. coeff.	All countries (Model 3)	Minimum coefficient	Country omitted at min. coeff.
Lagged DV	0.871*** [.024]	Portugal	0.863*** [0.022]	0.848*** [.019]	Iceland
Single-member district	−2.284*** [.519]	UK	−1.727*** [0.493]	−0.879* [.547]	New Zealand
Real per capita GDP	.0004*** [.0001]	Luxembourg	0.0003*** [0.0001]	.0002*** [.0000]	Iceland
Imports as a share of GDP	−0.143*** [.0198]	New Zealand	−0.1266*** [0.0173]	−0.080*** [.010]	Iceland
Population, log	−2.213*** [.378]	New Zealand	−1.8375*** [0.3136]	−0.844*** [.130]	Iceland
GDP growth rate	−.265*** [.083]	Iceland	−0.0904 [0.1290]	−.050 [.131]	Japan
Change in exchange rate	−0.830*** [.029]	Iceland	−0.6723*** [0.0415]	−0.655*** [.041]	Japan
U.S. Inflation rate	0.108 [.140]	Iceland	−0.0264 [0.1898]	−0.061 [.193]	Italy

Note: The maximum and the minimum are defined in terms of absolute value. Panel-corrected standard errors in brackets. * if $p < 0.1$, ** if $p < 0.05$, *** if $p < 0.01$. All tests are two-tailed.

Next, to ensure that our empirical results are not driven by any particular country, we follow Kittel and Winner (2005) and perform a Jackknife analysis (Elton and Tibshirani 1993; Gentle 2002) on our Model 4. Specifically, we reestimate the model repeatedly, excluding one country in each run. The resulting minimum and maximum values of the estimates of key co-variates are presented in Table 3.2. We can clearly see that the coefficient of SMD remains negative and significant throughout, even under this demanding procedure.

Finally, we test our electoral systems hypothesis against other competing theories in the political economy literature. Indeed, even should we succeed in controlling for all possible confounders and, additionally, should we nevertheless continue to estimate a robust effect of electoral systems on real prices, we still will not have distinguished between several mechanisms by which electoral systems could yield lower price levels. Multiple governmental and electoral features co-vary with electoral system, any one of which could alone or in combination affect prices.

First, systematic differences between electoral systems in the provision of state funding for and spending caps on election campaigns could alter politicians' responsiveness to organized producers. As Denzau and Munger (1986) demonstrate in their model of how politicians optimize their allocation of effort between organized interest groups (read: producers) that provide electoral resources and unorganized interests (read: consumers) that provide only votes, resources attract legislators' favor. Extending this model to nomination procedures under different electoral systems, Bawn and Thies (2003) find that legislators favor organized interests more under (closed list) PR than SMD. This, however, is a marginal effect: we, of course, are also interested in levels.

Setting aside different marginal effects of producer resources such as campaign donations on legislative favor, differences in the amount of campaign donations legally permitted may also matter. Greater governmental regulation and financing of campaigns could theoretically reduce producer resources, weaken producers vis-à-vis consumers, and offset the previous marginal effect. Hence, we utilize the Political Finance Database provided by the International IDEA.[26] We focus especially on two important indexes of governmental regulation and financing of campaigns – whether political parties receive direct public funding and whether there exists a ceiling on party election expenditure. In search of parsimony, we build a composite variable, *RESTRICT*, by taking the average of these two indexes. We remain agnostic about whether the greater marginal effect or smaller sum of producer contributions in PR systems has the greater effect on legislative attentions. A large net effect in either direction, however, cannot be ignored.

Powell and Whitten (1993) offer a second alternative mechanism, certainly strongly associated with electoral system. To explain the instability of the economic vote estimated in cross-national election studies (cf. Paldam 1991), they argue that institutional arrangements clarify or obscure

---

[26] See www.idea.int/parties/finance/db/. Note that Greece and Luxembourg are not covered in this database and hence are dropped from this part of our analysis.

the responsibility of governing parties for policy outcomes. Voters hold high-clarity governments accountable for policy outcomes but cannot assign blame or credit as easily when multiple parties have hands on the wheel. We note that many of the components that increase clarity of responsibility, including those introduced by subsequent research (*inter alia,* Whitten and Palmer (1999) and Nadeau, Niemi, and Yoshinaka (2002)), are associated with majoritarian electoral arrangements: majority governments, single-party governments, absence of proportional committee systems, a low number of parties in government, ideological cohesion of governing parties. Single-party governments, which commonly emerge in SMD systems, understand that voters will punish or reward them – not a coalition member – for changes in the purchasing power of their income. Accountability, in turn, may tilt legislators' favors from producers to consumers. Entertaining this rival mechanism that might be driving a spurious relationship between electoral systems and price levels, we construct a dummy variable that takes the value of one in countries with high levels of clarity of responsibility.[27]

Model 8 provides a level playing field for these three competing hypotheses. As we can see, the positive and significant coefficient on campaign regulation, contrary to

---

[27] Luxembourg, Portugal, Spain, and Iceland are not covered in Powell and Whitten's study.

expectations, suggests that countries with stricter regulation of campaign finance are also associated with *higher* price levels. It is possible that campaign finance regulations and prices might both be determined by an omitted variable but, whatever this might be, it is not the electoral system. As of the year 2000, thirteen of fourteen PR and six of seven SMD states offered direct state funding of political campaigns. Campaign spending caps vary more across electoral systems – three of fourteen PR and four of seven SMD states imposed them in 2000 – but the stability of the SMD coefficient in Model 7 suggests that campaign finance regulations have little systematic association with electoral system. While the regulation of campaign spending has a significant and positive effect that contradicts the expectations of the campaign finance rival hypothesis, the coefficient on clarity of responsibility simply reveals no significant effect, and seems not to impose any consequence on prices. Despite controls for rival mechanisms, a majoritarian electoral system remains a crucial institutional force that suppresses price levels.

During the course of our empirical inquiry, we remained cautious about issues of autocorrelation. As astute readers will have noted, estimates of the coefficient of the lagged dependent hover around 0.85 across all models. This alerts us that the lagged dependent variable alone may fail to handle adequately the autocorrelation that underlies the data-generating process. To address this concern, we follow the standard practice and estimate a first difference model. The results in Model 9 (Table 3.5) show that the change of electoral system (i.e., a shift from PR to SMD) does reduce the price after a one-year lag. In this specification, all variables enter the regression in the form of first differences. The first-differenced SMD variable (ΔSMD) is also entered with a one-year lag (ΔSMD$_{t-1}$), because we suspect that a shift from PR to SMD systems might take time to register its effect on the price. We find that the unlagged first-differenced SMD variable has the correct sign but is only marginally significant. However, the lagged first-differenced SMD variable is significant at less than the .05 level; the value of the coefficient is -3.52, indicating that a shift from PR systems to SMD systems is associated with a reduction of the change in price level by 3.3 percent.

This result suggests more complex dynamics than a first-difference model can provide. Moreover, because our key independent variable SMD varies only in France, Japan, Italy, and New Zealand over the period we consider, the first-difference approach would provide too little variation to test our hypothesis adequately. Therefore, we re-cast our model into a single-equation error correction form (ECM) to estimate the long-run relationship and the short-run dynamics simultaneously.[28] Notice that while the ECM and the

---

[28] Concretely, the single equation ECM regresses the first difference of the dependent variable on (1) its lagged level and any lagged changes

Table 3.5. Robustness checks: First differenced and error correction models

	Model 9: First differenced	Model 10: ECM
Lagged dependent variable		−.046***
		[.014]
△ Single-member district	−2.072	−.282
	[1.676]	[1.257]
△ Single-member district, lag	−3.522**	
	[1.760]	
Single-member district, lag		−.970**
		[.392]
△ Real per capita GDP	.004***	.004***
	[.000]	[.000]
Real per capita GDP, lag		−.000
		[.000]
△ Imports as a share of GDP	.162	.168
	[.221]	[.120]
Imports as a share of GDP, lag		−.057***
		[.011]
△ Population, log	16.942	67.446*
	[53.615]	[35.129]
Population, log, lag		−.775***
		[.174]
△ GDP growth rate	−.228*	−.528***
	[.126]	[.082]
GDP growth rate, lag		−.416***
		[.096]
△ Change in exchange rate	−.219***	−.331***
	[.044]	[.035]
Change in exchange rate, lag		−.281***
		[.034]

Electoral Systems and Real Prices

	Model 9: First differenced	Model 10: ECM
Δ U.S. Inflation rate	.889***	−.187
	[.283]	[.164]
U.S. Inflation rate, lag		−.786***
		[.138]
Constant	−3.190	
	[.787]	
Joint significance of fixed effects		.000***
N	643	643

Note: Panel-corrected standard errors in brackets. * p < 0.1, ** p < 0.05, *** p < 0.01. All tests are two-tailed. The decade coefficients (including the constant) in Model 10 are omitted in the interest of space.

auto-distributed lag models (where the lagged dependent variable model can be seen as a special case) are mathematically equivalent,[29] an important advantage of the ECM is that it avoids a spurious relationship because its dependent variable is first-differenced.

suggested by the data as necessary to pick up the auto-correlation components, (2) lagged values of potential cointegrating independent variables, and (3) whatever changes in the independent variables are suggested by the theory. The coefficients on first-differenced independent variables represent "transitory effects" of changes in independent variables on changes in the dependent variable; coefficients on lagged independent variables represent "permanent relationships" between levels of the independent and dependent variables (Franzese 2002). Because we do not have any theoretical prior belief about whether the effects of the explanatory variables are temporary or persistent, we include all explanatory variables in both contemporaneous differences and lagged terms.

[29] A recent study by DeBoef and Keele (2006) provides strong evidence using a Monte Carlo simulation.

The results are reported in Model 10. Note that the coefficient on PPP/XR_{t-1} reflects the dynamics of the relationship between co-variates and price levels, and its estimated coefficient, $-.046$, implies a considerably slower adjustment process than did our simple lagged dependent variable (LDV) model. Specifically, more than 95 percent $(1 + (-.046))$ of a shock to price level in the current year will last into the next. In addition, the result indicates that for half of a price shock's long-run impact to emerge will require almost fourteen years, rather than the four to seven years suggested by the LDV model.[30] More importantly, note that the coefficient on SMD_{t-1} is negative and significant. The estimate of the long-run effect of a permanent change from PR to SMD systems is thus $(-.970)/-(-.046) = -21.08$, which again supports, and indeed strengthens, our hypothesis: in the long run, real price levels are lower under SMD than under PR systems by more than 15 percent $(21.08/105.6 = 19.96)$. We suspect that this estimate of time to reequilibration, and perhaps also of long-term effect, is closer to reality than that of our LDV model. In addition, the corroborating evidence from the ECM model should further alleviate any lingering concern regarding the potential threat of the unit roots.

In sum, all the analyses presented so far, including checks for robustness against most (but, obviously, not all)

---

[30] $-\log2/\log(.954) = 14.71$.

conceivable sources of estimation error, underscore our basic result: real prices are indeed lower under SMD systems. Controlling for wealth, trade barriers, population size, GDP growth rate, exchange rate fluctuations, and the inflation rate in the United States, SMD electoral systems are associated with at least a 10 percent drop in real prices, and likely an even larger one, in the average OECD country.

III. Discussion and Conclusion

The model laid out in Chapter 2 strongly suggests that governmental policy will be biased toward consumers under almost all majoritarian electoral systems, toward producers – or, more generally, toward organized interests – under systems of PR; and one clear manifestation of this bias will be higher real price levels under PR, lower prices under majoritarian systems. The empirical analysis undergirding this claim, however, has been limited to a cross-section of the OECD countries for a single year presented in the original Rogowski and Kayser (2002) paper, which could do little more than establish the plausibility of the hypothesis. Evidence for the OECD countries over a period of thirty years presented here now bears out the theoretical expectation, both cross-sectionally and over time, with considerable robustness and under a much greater variety of statistical tests: SMD electoral systems are associated with lower prices; and hence, we conclude, also with greater consumer power. Moreover, we are able to establish, as the earlier study did not: (a) the likely effects of a change of electoral system in a single county and (b) the short- versus long-term impact and the length of time required to reach the new equilibrium. We attach particular importance to the present finding that the long-term effects of electoral systems are at least as strong as the cross-sectional ones that the earlier study established. Finally, the present study, by exploiting the fortuitous fact that several OECD countries changed electoral systems in the 1980s and 1990s, substantially remedies problems of systematic differences between PR and SMD systems.

Obviously, more questions remain, not least about endogenous institutions and the role of electoral competitiveness. Consider endogenous institutions: While this chapter treats the electoral system as exogenous, one might reasonably suspect that policy outcomes induced by alternative electoral systems in turn shape voters' preferences about the choice of electoral systems. Put differently, while this chapter shows that PR (majoritarian) systems systematically lead to higher (lower) prices and higher socioeconomic equality (inequality), it might well be the case that voters in societies characterized by greater equality (inequality) are motivated to support PR (majoritarian) systems. In this sense, electoral systems could be self-sustaining, and the self-reinforcing cycle between the choice of electoral system and social equality may provide a previously unnoticed account for institutional stability. We address precisely this possibility in Chapter 6.

No less important a topic for future research is the role of electoral competitiveness. Readers of Chapter 2 will recall that the seats-votes elasticities are predicated on an equal division of the vote. Once a single party in a majoritarian system becomes sufficiently dominant, the price predictions of the model actually reverse. That is, majoritarian countries with a traditionally dominant party can expect higher prices than they would have had under PR. Investigating the precise role of electoral competitiveness in mediating or moderating the relationship between electoral systems and real price levels promises considerable gains.

These and other questions call for investigation. However, we take it by now as at least highly likely that, among the economically advanced democracies, more majoritarian systems produce policies markedly friendlier to consumers, and less favorable to producers, than do systems of proportional representation.

4

Electoral Systems and Real Prices around the World

W e have proposed that a democracy's electoral rules are linked to the regulatory output of that country's elected legislators, and that this effect manifests itself in a country's real-price levels. In particular, we contend that the greater seat-vote elasticities of majoritarian electoral systems will tilt policy in favor of consumers, while proportional systems should strengthen producers; and that the pro-consumer bias of majoritarian systems should lead to systematically lower prices.

Empirical testing of our hypothesis in Chapter 3 supported the expected relationship between majoritarian electoral institutions and lower real prices among the wealthy, developed democracies of the Organization for Economic Cooperation and Development (OECD). Among the twenty-three OECD democracies, a country that shifted from a proportional to a majoritarian electoral system was estimated typically to enjoy a short-run yearly reduction in real prices of about 1.2 index points (where U.S. prices = 100), corresponding to a long-run reduction in real prices of at least 10 percent. This is about half of a standard deviation of average prices across OECD countries – over time, a significant effect.

However, OECD democracies represent only approximately one quarter of all democracies worldwide, and they differ in significant ways from democracies outside the OECD – above all, in levels of wealth. In the year 2000, the average per capita GDP of an OECD member country was six times greater than that of an average non-OECD democracy. Even though wealth is the leading predictor of real-price levels cross-nationally (Rogoff 1996), our model makes no distinction between rich and poor democracies. Therefore, the empirical question remains: will electoral systems have the same price effects in economically less developed democracies? Not necessarily, and indeed there are good reasons *ex ante* to conjecture that the effects might even be reversed.

For a variety of reasons, political institutions tend to be weaker in poorer societies, and perhaps weakest of all in poor democracies. The very regulatory mechanisms that affect competition and prices in economically advanced democracies might have little effect in poorer ones, or at any rate the marginal effects of electoral systems might be overwhelmed by the usual plethora of poorer-county problems: corruption, instability, frequent reversions to authoritarian rule (Adserá, Boix, and Payne 2003; Przeworski et al. 2000; Treisman 2000;

Mauro 1995). Even more problematic, an extensive literature suggests why, in at least a considerable subset of poorer countries, consumers might actually prefer higher real prices in the form of an appreciated currency – and hence, in terms both of our theory and of the Stigler-Peltzman framework on which it relies, why an electoral system that increased consumer power might actually raise prices rather than lowering them (Frieden and Stein 2001; Leblang 1999; Frieden 1991). Testing our theory only in the OECD, therefore, is not enough.

In this chapter, we broaden our analysis to span the complete population of all democracies worldwide, from 1972 to 2000. Very specifically, we ask: all else equal, are real-price levels actually lower, over time and cross-nationally, in democracies with majoritarian electoral institutions than in democracies that elect by proportionality? Were we to examine all democracies worldwide and find no electoral system effect on prices, our theory would at a minimum require qualification.

In fact, this is not what we find at all. This chapter provides the strongest evidence yet that, in addition to their political and macroeconomic effects, electoral systems also have policy effects, as legislators regulate to vie for the electoral support of producers versus consumers. To preview our results, we estimate the effect of electoral system on real prices worldwide to be worth between two and three index points yearly, corresponding to a long-run difference of more than 10 percent, in the expected direction.

Why Might Our Theory Break Down Outside the OECD?

Variation in the seats-votes elasticity of a country's electoral system, as argued earlier, affects legislators' incentives to favor either the interests of consumers or those of producers when formulating economic regulation. As the share of legislative seats won by any particular political party becomes increasingly sensitive to small changes in the aggregate national vote, consumers (*qua* voters) are empowered over producers, and legislators are exposed to increased electoral pressure to implement regulatory policies that keep the prices of goods and services low. In contrast, lower seats-votes elasticities give parties greater flexibility to appeal to producers over consumers; thus predicting higher consumer prices – and, in the short term, greater producer profits.

A country's "real" price level is the U.S. dollar equivalent of a generic basket of goods in that country. It is calculated (as noted earlier) simply as the cost or "purchasing power parity" (PPP) of those goods in local currency, divided by that country's exchange rate (XR) with the United States. This ratio of a country's PPP to XR standardizes price measures for cross-national comparison.

In the OECD, policy debates over market regulation predominantly determine the value of PPP. Yet consider a typical poor-country scenario that involves production almost entirely for export, with virtually all consumer goods being imported. Examples include Brazil and Ghana in their heyday as the world's leading producers of coffee and cocoa, respectively; early twentieth-century Argentina (exporting chiefly meat and wheat, importing from Britain virtually everything else it consumed); Chile when exports of copper ore dominated its whole economic life; and almost every major petroleum-exporting country.

In such a situation, as Jeffry Frieden has emphasized in general and Robert Bates (1997; 14–15, 33–36) has illuminated in the particular case of Brazil, the country's exchange rate almost inevitably becomes a dominant political issue, producers favoring a depreciated currency and consumers an appreciated one. The logic is simple: when coffee beans sold for $1 a pound on world markets, Brazilian coffee producers wanted each of those dollars to translate into as many *réis* as possible; but Brazilian consumers wanted each *real* to trade for the greatest possible number of dollars, so as to buy imported goods most cheaply. In the usual economic terms, however, all else being equal a depreciated exchange rate (a large XR) denotes lower real prices, while an appreciated (or small) XR denotes higher real prices.

This perverse result, exactly the opposite of what would obtain in a more diversified economy, means that political institutions that augment consumer power very well might lead to an appreciated exchange rate (and raise real prices), while ones that increase producer power would depreciate the exchange rate (and lower real prices).[1] For these export-dependent economies, then, we would expect if anything that majoritarian electoral systems would entail higher real prices; and, admitting that such economies are a considerable fraction of the whole set of less developed countries, we might reasonably expect at a minimum some attenuation, at a maximum a reversal of the majoritarian-low prices link that we observed in the economically advanced democracies.

Democracies and Electoral Systems Worldwide

The number of countries under democratic rule worldwide has risen steadily over the past thirty years. To begin our analysis, we partition the world's countries into democracies and nondemocracies using two rigorous and widely accepted – but distinct – rating methodologies: the annual Freedom House measure of "political rights" (Freedom House 2004) and the annual Polity IV Project "combined polity score" (Marshall and Jaggers 2002). Both methods assign every country in the world a yearly, ordinal score measuring the presence or absence of various aspects of democratic governance: free, regular, and competitive elections, meaningful political

---

[1] This pattern extended, in the Latin American cases, to democracy itself. Typically the authoritarian regimes, which entrenched the power of economically concentrated producers (particularly landowners), kept the local currency depreciated, while under episodes of democracy the exchange rate was kept artificially high.

opposition, universal suffrage, and so forth.[2] Countries rated 1 or 2 on the 7-point Freedom House scale, and 6 or greater on the Polity IV scale (which ranges from -10 to $+10$) are generally considered to be democratic.[3]

The Freedom House and Polity IV scores, while highly correlated, are not interchangeable. They employ different methodologies, and the use of either may produce substantively divergent results (see Casper and Tufis 2003; Munck and Verkuilen 2002). Most significantly, countries and years identified as democratic by Freedom House are not always identified as democratic by Polity IV, and vice versa.[4] We therefore err on the side of caution and perform separate analyses on

---

[2] While there exist multiple definitions of what exactly constitutes a democracy (see Przeworski et al. [2000], ch. 1 for a thorough review), these factors capture the most widely agreed-upon criteria. Note that some, particularly Elkins (2000) and Treier and Jackman (2003) have cautioned against the measurement of "democracy" as a dichotomy, preferring continuous or latent measures to capture gradations of democratic features of governance. As we are only interested in measuring democracy for the purpose of selecting a sample, however, a dichotomous measure is appropriate to our methodology.

[3] Examples of other studies in political science employing these rules include, for *Freedom House*, Tavits (2005), Barro (1999), Blais and Dobrzynska (1998), and Bollen (1993); and for *Polity IV*, Li (2006), Blais, Dobrzynska, and Indridason (2004), and Dixon (1994).

[4] One notable example is Poland in1990. Whereas *Freedom House* considers Poland to have been democratic in 1990, *Polity IV* codes Poland as not becoming democratic until 1991. Arguably, *Polity IV* provides the superior measure here. In Poland's 1989 parliamentary election, only 35 percent of the seats were competitive; the rest were reserved for the Communist Party. A fully competitive parliamentary election was not held until 1991.

the two similar but not identical populations of democracies as identified by each coding system.

Our analysis spans the years from 1972 to 2000. Over this interval, a few countries were democracies for such a short period of time that we would not realistically expect any relationship between electoral system and real prices to obtain. We therefore filter from our data sets country-years with very brief (only one or two years at a time) spells of democracy. We also drop a small number of countries with five or fewer total years of democratic rule in this twenty-nine year span. Taken together, these restrictions turn out to be fairly noninvasive. The resultant Freedom House data set includes 1671 country-years of democracy, spanning 90 different countries, and the Polity IV data set includes 1,467 country-years of democracy, spanning 76 different countries.

For each of these democracies, we again measure electoral system elasticity, as before, as a dichotomous indicator of whether a country employs majoritarian or proportional electoral rules, reflecting the central divide between the world's electoral systems (Lijphart 1999; Powell 2000). Majoritarian electoral systems are distinguished by their use of winner-take-all, single- member legislative districts (SMD), typically decided by either majority or plurality vote. Proportional systems, on the other hand, employ multimember legislative districts in which two or more winners are selected in proportion to the vote outcome of each district. By design,

proportional systems have extremely low seats-votes elasticities in the neighborhood of one. Majoritarian systems, in contrast, introduce much greater distortion into the seats-votes
function at the district level, and thus have more potential for
large changes in seat share given relatively smaller changes in
vote share.[5]

To code the electoral system variable, we rely on Colomer's
(2004) *Handbook of Electoral System Choice* and Golder's
(2005) data set of world electoral systems.[6] Countries with
only SMDs we code as majoritarian (1), and countries with
only multimember legislative districts we code as proportional (0).[7] A handful of democracies employ mixed electoral
systems that elect legislators using both single-and multimember districts. In these cases, if a country allocates more
than half of its seats in SMD and the overall seat allocation
rule is either parallel or two-tiered (with the single-member
and multimember district seats allocated separately, and at

---

[5] Exceptions to the rule of high levels of majoritarian system elasticity may
occur when the overall number of electoral districts is small, as elections
become less competitive, or as partisan gerrymanders create many safe
seats.

[6] These references were further cross-checked against the World Bank's
Database of Political Institutions (Beck, Clarke, Groff, Keefer, and Walsh
2001).

[7] Following this rule, Japan's single nontransferable vote and Mongolia's
block voting systems are coded as proportional; that is, as having a seats-
votes elasticity more similar to proportional systems than to majoritarian
systems. Recoding these two countries as majoritarian only strengthens
the significance of our findings.

least one of the tiers employing SMD), then we consider that country to be majoritarian. Otherwise, if half or more of the seats are allocated in multimember districts, or if more than half of the seats are elected in SMD but the overall seat allocation rule is proportional, then we consider that country to be proportional.[8]

In sum, our data sets contain a large amount of information about democracies outside the OECD, with non-OECD democracies representing approximately 60 percent of the cases. Even in the early years of the study, the population is never dominated by the OECD. By electoral system, approximately one-third of the observed country-years are majoritarian (Table 4.1).

Of the countries included in either the Freedom House or Polity IV data sets, only ten ever switched between majoritarian and proportional electoral systems during the time period under investigation: France, Italy, Japan, and New Zealand within the OECD, and Latvia, Mongolia, Poland (assuming it was democratic in 1990), Sri Lanka, Thailand, and Ukraine outside the OECD. In addition, there were five countries – Bolivia, Bulgaria, Lithuania, Madagascar, and

---

[8] For more on this distinction, see the useful glossary of Colomer (2004), particularly pp. 550–551. The system of mixed single- and multimember electoral districts with overall proportional allocation of seats is occasionally termed "personalized proportional representation," "compensatory allocation," or "mixed member proportional." Examples include Germany, Venezuela, and postelectoral reform New Zealand.

Table 4.1. Distribution of cases among OECD and non-OECD democracies in the two data sets. Majoritarian systems are denoted SMD and proportional systems are denoted PR. Mixed systems are allocated as described in the text

| | Freedom House data set | | | |
	PR	SMD	% SMD	Total
OECD	475	181	27.6	656
Non-OECD	557	458	45.1	1015
Total	1032	639	38.2	1671
	Polity IV data set			
	PR	SMD	% SMD	Total
OECD	415	181	30.4	596
Non-OECD	573	298	34.2	871
Total	988	479	32.7	1467

Venezuela – that adopted mixed electoral rules without altering the basic majoritarian/proportional orientation of the preceding system.

Global Trends and Explaining Variation in Real Prices

The dependent variable in this study is the real price level of GDP, measured both cross-nationally and over time. Following the Penn World Tables (PWT) 6.1 (Heston, Summers, and Aten 2002), from which we draw price level data, the United States is selected as a baseline country with real price levels

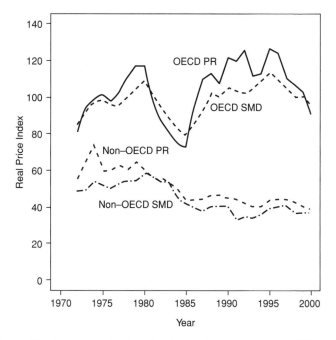

Figure 4.1. Average real prices by electoral system among OECD and non-OECD democracies in Polity IV data set, 1972–2000. Each trend line represents only the central tendency of prices; around each mean value, the standard deviation in each subgroup, each year, is approximately twenty index points.

fixed at 100 in all years. Other countries' price levels are then calculated as the domestic price level of GDP, divided by the U.S. exchange rate, times 100.

Real price levels exhibit a great deal of variation both across country and over time (Figure 4.1). In devising a series of models to explain this variation, we focus especially on the massive gap in real prices between rich and poor democracies, to test whether the effect of electoral systems on price levels is conditioned by variation in levels of wealth.

As in earlier chapters, we include statistical controls for one-year lagged real prices, per capita GDP, imports as a percent of GDP, population size, the change in yearly exchange rates with the U.S. dollar, and the U.S. inflation rate.[9] A country's real price level changes continually over time as a function of its two constituent measures: domestic price levels and exchange rates with the United States. Controlling for real price levels in the previous year captures the bulk of this dynamic, and ensures that the explanatory effect of the other independent variables on yearly real price levels is not over-estimated in our regression models.

How a country's wealth drives up its real price levels was first explicated by Balassa (1964) and Samuelson (1964), and wealth has been extensively confirmed as the strongest predictor of price levels cross-nationally (see also Rogoff 1996; Bergstrand 1991; Bhagwati 1984; and Kravis and Lipsey 1983). Because the variance in per capita GDP over time is greater

---

[9] The literature on explaining cross-national variation in real price levels stems primarily from empirical testing of the theory of the "Law of One Price," which claims that cross-national differences in real price levels should be systematically eliminated over short periods of time through the process of arbitrage. In reality, this "law" only holds in highly attenuated form (see for example Rogoff 1996; Bergstrand 1991; Kravis and Lipsey 1988; and Clague 1986).

in wealthier countries, per capita GDP describes a curvilinear relationship with real price levels.

Economic openness to trade, as measured by the value of a country's imports as a percent of GDP, is expected to correlate with lower real price levels, as it increases opportunities for arbitrage and reflects reduced state ability or will to maintain abnormally high price levels. Large population size is likewise expected to push down real price levels, by increasing opportunities for market specialization and by producing economies of scale.

Controlling for yearly changes in exchange rates accounts for an important time dynamic in the dependent variable. Because exchange rates fluctuate more rapidly than do domestic price levels, we expect recent currency depreciations to lead to short-term decreases in the real price level, and vice versa. The coefficient on the change in exchange rates should therefore be negative.[10]

Lastly, the fact that global real prices are indexed to the United States requires that some corrective be employed to control for the fact that increasing United States inflation

[10] Currency depreciation from one year to the next is revealed by an increase in the number of units of local currency required to "purchase" one U.S. dollar. Recall that, by construction, real price levels are calculated with exchange rates in the denominator, so that unless currency depreciations (i.e., increases in the denominator) are matched by identical and immediate price increases in the numerator – which they typically are not – then the effects will fail to offset, and real prices will drop. Obviously, the reverse is also the case.

weakens the U.S. dollar against foreign currencies. Regardless of what is happening abroad, if the dollar weakens, real prices outside the United States will appear to decrease even if, for the domestic consumer, price levels remain constant. Therefore we expect the coefficient on this variable to be negative.[11]

In addition to the price level data that we obtain from the PWT 6.1, we obtain U.S. inflation rate and per capita GDP data from the International Monetary Fund World Economic Outlook database, and data on the remaining control variables from the World Bank World Development Indicators data set.

Testing the Electoral System Effect

With many more countries than years observed, our data sets are time-series cross-sections (TSCS). As Beck and Katz (2004, 27) note, "There is no mechanical solution ... for dealing with TSCS data; analysts must think about how to model their particular data." To test our theory in the OECD countries, we applied ordinary least squares with panel-corrected standard errors (OLS-PCSE; see Beck and Katz 1995). The coefficient on

---

[11] The U.S. inflation rate tracks closely with the U.S. current account balance as percent of GDP, for which there are also reasons to expect a price effect. Current-account deficits represent the willingness of foreign countries to subsidize consumption in the United States, which imply higher real prices in the United States with respect to the rest of the world. Using this variable instead of the inflation rate in the models produces nearly identical results.

the electoral system variable was thus an estimate of how real price levels would change, *ceteris paribus*, if a country hypothetically switched between majoritarian and proportional electoral systems.

As the scope of our inquiry in this chapter is the entire population of democratic countries in the world, we are less interested in the conditional effect on real price levels of particular countries' switching between majoritarian and proportional electoral systems – a rare event, regardless – but rather in drawing inferences about marginal group differences between majoritarian and proportional democracies. Based upon this theoretical distinction – and aided by a considerable increase in the amount of data under investigation in the world sample – we model the effect of electoral systems on real prices using the linear generalized estimating equation (GEE) method for a continuous dependent variable. This approach was originally set forth by Liang and Zeger (1986) and reviewed for applications in political science by Zorn (2001).[12]

The GEE method estimates the marginal effects of a series of co-variates on a dependent variable that is known to have clusters of correlated or repeated observations – here, real price levels that are correlated within countries over time.

---

[12] Concerning the differences between models of "conditional" effects such as OLS and models of "marginal" effects such as GEE, Agresti (2002) provides a particularly helpful discussion; see pp. 466–476 and 500–502.

It also permits the explicit modeling of time-dynamics of the dependent variable within each country. Because it is impossible, due to data limitations, to estimate precisely how prices are correlated within countries, over time,[13] we follow standard practice in positing and estimating the parameters of a series of simpler "working" correlation structures. We then assess each model's efficiency and success at fitting the data.[14] We find that assuming exchangeability in the across-year correlation structure produces the best model. This means that each year's real price levels are assumed to be correlated equally with every other year's real price levels for every given country.[15] The correlation parameter σ is estimated as part of fitting the model.

Figure 4.2 illustrates the GEE model as applied to the simpler bivariate relationship between real price levels and the square root of per capita GDP. Each thin line represents the OLS fit for one country to the within-country observations for these two variables. Very few of these lines – particularly

---

[13] The maximum number of years observed for each country is 29. A correlation matrix of yearly prices is symmetric, so to estimate a 29-year-by-29-year correlation matrix would require estimating 406 pairwise correlation parameters. We do not have nearly enough data to estimate reliably this many parameters.

[14] For each working model, we estimate both naïve and robust standard errors to evaluate alternate correlation structures. In GEE models, robust standard error estimates are consistent even if the assumed working correlation structure is erroneous (Diggle, Liang, and Zeger 1994).

[15] Rejected correlation structures include an autocorrelation model (about which we say more later) and a multiple-period stationarity model.

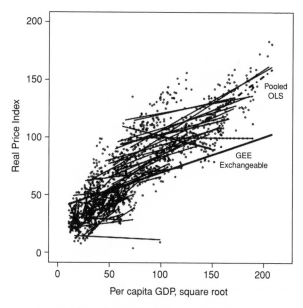

Figure 4.2. Scatterplot of real price levels against square root transformed per capita GDP in democracies in the Polity IV data set, 1972–2000. Each point represents one country-year. The scatterplot is overlaid with three types of best-fit lines, for the bivariate relationship. The multiple thin solid lines are the within-country linear fits; these lines span the length of the observed range of per capita GDP in each respective country. The thick dashed line is the pooled OLS best fit, ignoring the within-country correlation of real price levels across time. The thick solid line is the GEE best fit, assuming an exchangeable correlation structure.

at the low end of per capita GDP, where countries exhibit little over-time variation – run parallel to the pooled ordinary least squares best fit line. This reveals significant cross-country heterogeneity but also shows that the pooled OLS fit, which wrongly assumes that all observations are independent, is overestimating the actual effect of per capita GDP on real price levels. A better estimate of the relationship between these variables is given by the linear GEE model assuming an exchangeable within-country correlation structure, which runs visibly parallel to many more of the within-country fits.

In Table 4.2, the baseline model gives the results from estimating the linear exchangeable GEE model as specified earlier. Note that in all of the models, the signs on the control variables are as expected. The effect of having a majoritarian electoral system is estimated to decrease real price levels by approximately two points on the price index. This estimate is slightly higher and statistically significant at the 2 percent level in the Freedom House data set, and slightly lower and statistically significant at the 6 percent level in the Polity IV data set.

To test whether this electoral system effect is being driven by the experience of the world's wealthiest democracies, we next add an interaction between the electoral system and GDP variables to the model. We find no statistically significant interaction effect, and in substantive terms, the estimated effect is nearly zero. In the Polity IV data, the model finds some attenuation in the electoral system effect in poorer democracies that does not appear in the Freedom House data. But in both data sets, the overall significance of electoral systems remains the same. The long-term decrease in price levels

Table 4.2. Linear GEE models, assuming exchangeability; robust standard errors in parentheses. Dependent variable is real price level. Models labeled "No mixed ES" exclude democratic country-years with mixed majoritarian-proportional electoral systems. Models labeled "Imputed" are results from averaging more than ten GEE models fit to imputed data sets; all other models employ listwise deletion. Per capita GDP has been re-centered in models other than Baseline to maintain a consistent interpretation of its coefficient estimate

	Freedom House				Polity IV			
	Baseline	Interaction	No mixed ES	Imputed	Baseline	Interaction	No mixed ES	Imputed
Majoritarian electoral system	-2-236	-2.241	-3-475	-2.020	-1.705	-1.604	-2.944	-2.207
	(0.919)	(0.898)	(0.965)	(1.103)	(0.911)	(0.910)	(1.013)	(0.914)
Lagged real prices	0.744	0.745	0.735	0.576	0.690	0.689	0.674	0.698
	(0.047)	(0.047)	(0.052)	(0.073)	(0.048)	(0.048)	(0.053)	(0.046)
Per capita GDP (square root)	0.105	0.105	0.110	0.202	0.144	0.149	0.159	0.141
	(0.030)	(0.031)	(0.035)	(0.048)	(0.032)	(0.033)	(0.037)	(0.030)
Change in exchange rates (plus 0–3, natural log)	-8.825	-8.826	-8.581	-8.059	-6.862	-6.832	-6.621	-6.939
	(1.768)	(1.779)	(1.764)	(1.663)	(1.470)	(1.477)	(1.496)	(1.441)
Population (natural log)	-0.918	-0.919	-0.961	-0.908	-1.408	-1.393	-1.596	-0.954
	(0.394)	(0.392)	(0.449)	(0.657)	(0.475)	(0.483)	(0.592)	(0.459)

Imports as a percent of GDP	−0.170	−0.170	−0.175	−0.170	−0.211.	−0.211	−0.223	−0.164
	(0.040)	(0.041)	(0.044)	(0.048)	(0.046)	(0.047)	(0.053)	(0.045)
U.S. inflation rate	0.696	0.696	0.691	1.198	0.854	0.858	0.867	0.874
	(0.155)	(0.155)	(0.162)	(0.228)	(0.169)	(0.169)	(0.178)	(0.166)
SMD × GDP (square root)		0.001	−0.024	0.009		−0.013	−0.047	−0.005
		(0.020)	(0.019)	(0.029)		(0.021)	(0.021)	(0.020)
Constant	20.060	28.108	30.115	37.295	30.956	41.306	46.384	31.706
	(8.444)	(9.992)	(11.210)	(14.248)	(9.667)	(11.334)	(13–37)	(10.441)
Observations	1410	1410	1299	1652	1389	1389	1247	1459
ρ	0.247	0.247	0.279	0.295	0.289	0.286	0.344	0.230
Long-term SMD effect	−11.9%	−11.9%	−17.9%	−6.9%	−7.9%	−7.4%	−13.0%	−10.7%

attributable to a majoritarian electoral system is 12 percent in the Freedom House data set and 8 percent in the Polity IV data set.[16]

When countries employing mixed majoritarian-proportional electoral systems are excluded from the analysis, the electoral system effect becomes even more pronounced. Our initial coding rule partitioned mixed-system democracies according to whether they were more similar to pure majoritarian or proportional electoral systems. Yet, recall that the primary objective of our electoral system measure is to approximate seats-votes elasticity. Dividing up democracies that have more complex – and less well-understood – mixed systems in this manner may therefore introduce some measurement error into the analysis. In the models with mixed system democracies dropped, the estimated electoral system effect increases in significance to between three and three-and-a-half points, with a long-term effect of between 13 and 18 percent. Negative coefficients on the electoral system-wealth interaction term, indicating attenuation in the electoral system effect in poorer democracies, are now apparent in both data sets (although only statistically significant among the Polity IV countries). Holding all other control variables

---

[16] These values are for countries with average levels of wealth in the respective data sets. Long-term shifts are calculated as $\beta_{SND}/(1 - \beta_{iagn}))/\bar{p}$, where $\bar{p} = 73.42$ is the mean price level in the *Freedom House* data set and $\bar{p} = 69.29$ is the mean price level in the *Polity IV* data set.

Electoral Systems and Real Prices around the World

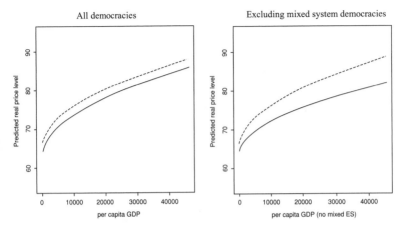

Figure 4.3. Predicted real price levels for democracies with majoritarian electoral systems (solid line) and proportional electoral systems (dashed line) at varying levels of per capita GDP. Using the results of the interaction (left) and no mixed ES (right) models in the Freedom House data set. All other control variables are held constant at their mean.

at their mean, however, this attenuation is not so great as to reverse the electoral system effect in less-wealthy democracies (Figure 4.3).

Each of our models thus far has employed listwise deletion, removing from the analysis all observations that contain missing values on either the dependent variable or any of the independent variables.[17] We guard against the potential

---

[17] The overall rate of missingness across these seven variables is 4.4% in the *Freedom House* data and 1% in the *Polity IV* data. Among only the dependent variable, real price levels, the rate of missingness in these two data sets is 13.2% and 3%, respectively.

for selection bias arising from this practice by applying the multiple imputation algorithm implemented in the software package Amelia II (Honaker, King, and Blackwell 2010; King, Honaker, Joseph, and Scheve 2001). The concern over bias is particularly acute in our analysis because 1) the variable measuring real price levels contains the most missing values; 2) poorer countries have more missing observations than wealthy countries; and 3) wealth is the primary known determinant of real price levels. The results of model-averaging the exchangeable GEE model across ten imputed data sets are given in the models labeled "imputed." The potential for bias resulting from nonrandomly missing observations is not realized. The magnitude of the coefficient on electoral system increases in the Polity IV model and decreases in the Freedom House model, but remains statistically significant at the 2 percent and 10 percent levels, respectively. These coefficients also remain well within the range of the nonimputed model coefficients, given the standard errors of both.

The preceding models have all sought to estimate the aggregate effect of majoritarian versus proportional electoral rules on real price levels between 1972 and 2000. We now test for the possibility that this aggregate effect might have arisen from the averaging out of otherwise irregular yearly shifts in price levels, with prices higher in some years under proportional electoral rules, and in other years (contrary to our theory) under majoritarian electoral rules. From Figure 4.1, it is not immediately apparent whether the posited electoral system effect increased, decreased, or remained constant during the time period under investigation. To address this question, we add two sets of year fixed-effects to the interaction model, one each for majoritarian and proportional democracies. The predicted yearly difference in price levels between the two electoral systems, once the effects of the other explanatory variables have been controlled for, can then be directly calculated from the coefficients on the electoral system dummy variable and the year-electoral system fixed effects.[18]

The results from this model confirm that higher real price levels are a persistent year-to-year feature of proportional democracies when compared to majoritarian democracies. All else equal, price levels are estimated to be lower in majoritarian democracies in twenty-one out of twenty-eight years in the Freedom House data and twenty out of twenty-eight

---

[18] Specifically, using 1973 as the reference year, the model is:

$$Price\ Level = \beta_0 + \beta_1 SMD + \beta_2 SMD \times Year_{1974} + \beta_3 PR \times Year_{1974}$$
$$+ \beta_4 SMD \times Year_{1975} + \beta_5 PR \times Year_{1975}$$
$$+ \cdots + \sum \beta_j Other\ controls + \varepsilon.$$

Thus, for example, holding constant the control variables, the electoral system effect for 1974 is equal to $\beta_1 + \beta_2 - \beta_3$. The variance of this estimate is $Var(\beta_1) + Var(\beta_2) + Var(\beta_3) - 2(Cov(\beta_1; \beta_2) - Cov(\beta_1; \beta_2) - Cov(\beta_2; \beta_3))$. Because the variable measuring U.S. inflation rate is country-invariant in any given year, it is left out of this model due to its perfect collinearity with the year dummy variables.

years in the Polity IV data.[19] Although only a third of the yearly differences are statistically significant in the predicted direction at the 5 percent level, the number of observations per year is also typically quite low, ranging from just thirty-one to eighty. The average yearly difference is around two and a quarter index points.

The five-year moving average in Figure 4.4 reveals that the electoral system effect first shrank when prices in proportional democracies fell in the early 1980s, and then shrank again more gradually throughout the 1990s following an increase in the late 1980s.[20] Although we find this over-time phenomenon extremely interesting from a substantive perspective, we offer no particular explanation for it.

Conclusion

This chapter has provided the strongest evidence so far supporting the relationship theorized previously linking majoritarian electoral institutions to lower real prices among democracies worldwide. In so doing, the chapter also lends additional empirical support to the preceding foundational theory of Stigler (1971) and Peltzman (1976).

---

[19] It is not twenty-nine years because 1972 is dropped; as the earliest year in the data set, it contains no observed value of the lagged dependent variable.

[20] This trend is less apparent in the noisier, untransformed year-to-year estimates.

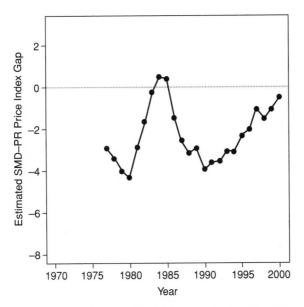

Figure 4.4. Yearly estimated difference in real price levels between majoritarian and proportional democracies in Polity IV data set, after controlling for GDP, changes in the exchange rate, population, and import levels: five-year moving average.

The value of this result is heightened due to the plausible reasons why the electoral system effect might not hold – or possibly even be reversed – in less-wealthy democracies. The original model captured key elements of the electoral linkage between voter preferences and regulatory output. In particular, majoritarian electoral systems that privilege consumers' over producers' preferences were expected to generate economic policy that favored consumers. But if, due to diminished state capacity, legislative action was a poor reflection of voter preference, then it would not be surprising to observe no electoral system effect in poorer democracies. Alternately, if legislators did regulate to favor consumers, but consumers preferred an appreciated exchange rate rather than a lower purchasing power parity – a logical response to living in a country whose economy depends on production almost entirely for export – then we would observe majoritarian electoral systems actually leading to higher real price levels. Neither of these turns out to be the case. The electoral system effect, while attenuated in poorer democracies, is never reversed.

Appendix
Countries and Years in Freedom House Data Set

The Freedom House data set is the population of countries and years identified as democratic by receiving a Freedom House "political rights" score of one or two between 1972 and 2000. Country-years corresponding to countries with very brief (only one or two years at a time) spells of democracy, and/or five or fewer total years of democratic government are not included. For electoral systems, SMD indicates single-member district majoritarian democracies; PR indicates multimember district proportional democracies; and, if labeled, Mixed indicates mixed systems. For each country, the total number of years of democracy included in our analysis from 1972 to 2000 is given in parenthesis.

Andorra (8): PR 1993–2000

Antigua and Barbuda (9): SMD 1981–1989

Argentina (17): PR 1973–1975, PR 1984–1997

Australia (29): SMD 1972–2000

Austria (29): PR 1972–2000

Bahamas (28): SMD 1973–2000

Bangladesh (7): SMD 1991–1994, SMD 1996–1998

Barbados (29): SMD 1972–2000

Belgium (29): PR 1972–2000

Belize (20): SMD 1981–2000

Benin (10): PR 1991–2000

Bolivia (20): PR 1981–1995, PR (Mixed) 1996–2000

Botswana (28): SMD 1973–2000

Brazil (10): PR 1986–1992, PR 1994–1996

Bulgaria (10): PR 1991–2000

Canada (29): SMD 1972–2000

Cape Verde (10): PR 1991–2000

Chile (8): PR 1990–1997

Colombia (20): PR 1972–1988, PR 1991–1993

Costa Rica (29): PR 1972–2000

Cyprus (20): PR 1981–2000

Czech Republic (8): PR 1993–2000

Denmark (29): PR 1972–2000

Dominica (23): SMD 1978–2000

Dominican Republic (18): PR 1978–1992, PR 1998–2000

Ecuador (18): PR 1979–1996

El Salvador (8): PR 1972–1975, PR 1997–2000

Estonia (6): PR 1995–2000

Fiji (15): SMD 1972–1986

Finland (29): PR 1972–2000

France (29): SMD 1972–1985, PR 1986–1987, SMD 1988–2000

Gambia, The (14): SMD 1972–1980, SMD 1989–1993

Germany (29): PR (Mixed) 1972–2000

Greece (27): PR 1974–2000

Grenada (21): SMD 1974–1978, SMD 1985–2000

Guyana (8): PR 1993–2000

Honduras (9): PR 1984–1992

Hungary (11): PR (Mixed) 1990–2000

Iceland (29): PR 1972–2000

India (24): SMD 1972–1990, SMD 1996–2000

Ireland (29): PR 1972–2000

Israel (29): PR 1972–2000

Italy (29): PR 1972–1992, SMD (Mixed) 1993–2000

Jamaica (29): SMD 1972–2000

Japan (29): PR 1972–1992, SMD (Mixed) 1993–2000

Kiribati (23): PR 1978–2000

Korea, South (13): SMD (Mixed) 1988–2000

Latvia (6): PR 1995–2000

Liechtenstein (9): PR 1992–2000

Lithuania (10): SMD 1991, SMD (Mixed) 1992–2000

Luxembourg (29): PR 1972–2000

Madagascar (8): PR 1993–1997, PR (Mixed) 1998–2000

Malta (29): PR 1972–2000

Marshall Islands (10): SMD 1991–2000

Mauritius (23): PR 1977–1979, PR 1981–2000

Micronesia (10): SMD 1991–2000

Monaco (8): PR 1993–2000

Mongolia (8): PR 1993–1995, SMD 1996–2000

Namibia (11): PR 1990–2000

Netherlands (29): PR 1972–2000

New Zealand (29): SMD 1972–1993, PR (Mixed) 1994–2000

Norway (29): PR 1972–2000

Palau (7): SMD 1994–2000

Panama (7): PR (Mixed) 1994–2000

Papua New Guinea (25): SMD 1976–2000

Peru (10): PR 1980–1989

Philippines (9): SMD (Mixed) 1987–1989, SMD (Mixed) 1995–2000

Poland (11): SMD 1990, PR 1991–2000

Portugal (25): PR 1976–2000

Samoa (12): PR 1989–2000

San Marino (14): PR 1972–1976, PR 1992–2000

Sao Tome and Principe (10): PR 1991–2000

Slovakia (7): PR 1994–2000

Slovenia (10): PR 1991–2000

Solomon Islands (22): SMD 1978–1999

South Africa (7): PR 1994–2000

Spain (24): PR 1977–2000

Sri Lanka (9): SMD 1972–1977, PR 1978–1980

St. Kitts and Nevis (20): SMD 1981–2000

St. Lucia (22): SMD 1979–2000

St. Vincent and Grenadines (22): SMD 1979–2000

Sweden (29): PR 1972–2000

Switzerland (29): PR 1972–2000

Trinidad and Tobago (29): SMD 1972–2000

Turkey (10): PR 1973–1979, PR 1990–1992

United Kingdom (29): SMD 1972–2000

United States (29): SMD 1972–2000

Uruguay (16): PR 1985–2000

Vanuatu (21): PR 1980–2000

Venezuela (23): PR 1972–1988, PR (Mixed) 1989–1991, PR (Mixed) 1996–1998

Countries and Years in Polity IV Data Set

The Polity IV data set is the population of countries and years identified as democratic by receiving a Polity IV "combined polity score" greater than or equal to six between 1972 and 2000. Country-years corresponding to countries with very brief (only one or two years at a time) spells of democracy, and/or five or fewer total years of democratic government are not included. For electoral systems, SMD indicates single-member district majoritarian democracies; PR indicates multimember district proportional democracies; and, if labeled, Mixed indicates mixed systems. For each country, the total number of years of democracy included in our analysis from 1972 to 2000 is given in parentheses.

Argentina (21): PR 1973–1975, PR 1983–2000
Australia (29): SMD 1972–2000
Austria (29): PR 1972–2000
Bangladesh (10): SMD 1991–2000
Belgium (29): PR 1972–2000
Benin (10): PR 1991–2000
Bolivia (19): PR 1982–1995, PR (Mixed) 1996–2000
Botswana (29): SMD 1972–2000
Brazil (16): PR 1985–2000
Bulgaria (11): PR (Mixed) 1990, PR 1991–2000
Canada (29): SMD 1972–2000
Chile (12): PR 1989–2000
Colombia (29): PR 1972–2000
Costa Rica (29): PR 1972–2000
Cyprus (29): PR 1972–2000
Czech Republic (11): PR 1990–2000
Denmark (29): PR 1972–2000

Dominican Republic (21): PR 1978–1993, PR 1996–2000

Ecuador (22): PR 1979–2000

El Salvador (17): PR 1984–2000

Estonia (10): PR 1991–2000

Fiji (15): SMD 1972–1986

Finland (29): PR 1972–2000

France (29): SMD 1972–1985, PR 1986–1987, SMD 1988–2000

Gambia, The (22): SMD 1972–1993

Germany (29): PR (Mixed) 1972–2000

Greece (26): PR 1975–2000

Guyana (9): PR 1992–2000

Honduras (15): PR 1982–1984, PR 1989–2000

Hungary (11): PR (Mixed) 1990–2000

India (29): SMD 1972–2000

Ireland (29): PR 1972–2000

Israel (29): PR 1972–2000

Italy (29): PR 1972–1992, SMD (Mixed) 1993–2000

Jamaica (29): SMD 1972–2000

Japan (29): PR 1972–1992, SMD (Mixed) 1993–2000

Korea, South (13): SMD (Mixed) 1988–2000

Latvia (10): SMD 1991, PR 1992–2000

Lithuania (10): SMD 1991, SMD (Mixed) 1992–2000

Macedonia (10): SMD (Mixed) 1991–2000

Madagascar (9): PR 1992–1997, PR (Mixed) 1998–2000

Malawi (7): SMD 1994–2000

Electoral Systems and Real Prices around the World

Mali (9): PR 1992–2000

Mauritius (29): PR 1972–2000

Moldova (8): PR 1993–2000

Mongolia (9): PR 1992–1995, SMD 1996–2000

Mozambique (7): PR 1994–2000

Namibia (11): PR 1990–2000

Netherlands (29): PR 1972–2000

New Zealand (29): SMD 1972–1993, PR (Mixed) 1994–2000

Nicaragua (11): PR 1990–2000

Norway (29): PR 1972–2000

Pakistan (15): SMD 1973–1976, SMD 1988–1998

Panama (12): PR (Mixed) 1989–2000

Papua New Guinea (26): SMD 1975–2000

Paraguay (9): PR 1992–2000

Peru (12): PR 1980–1991

Philippines (14): SMD (Mixed) 1987–2000

Poland (10): PR 1991–2000

Portugal (25): PR 1976–2000

Slovakia (8): PR 1993–2000

Slovenia (10): PR 1991–2000

Solomon Islands (22): SMD 1978–1999

South Africa (7): PR 1994–2000

Spain (23): PR 1978–2000

Sri Lanka (10): SMD 1972–1977, PR 1978–1981

Sweden (29): PR 1972–2000

Switzerland (29): PR 1972–2000

Thailand (9): PR 1992–1996, SMD (Mixed) 1997–2000

Trinidad and Tobago (29): SMD 1972–2000

Turkey (25): PR 1973–1979, PR 1983–2000

Ukraine (10): SMD 1991–1992, PR (Mixed) 1993–2000

United Kingdom (29): SMD 1972–2000

United States (29): SMD 1972–2000

Uruguay (16): PR 1985–2000

Venezuela (29): PR 1972–1988, PR (Mixed) 1989–1998, PR 1999–2000

5

A Closer Look: Case Studies and Mechanisms

In the previous chapters, we have focused on building a theory of how electoral incentives tilt regulatory policy – and hence, price levels – toward producers or consumers. We have also endeavored to construct a persuasive empirical case that real price levels are indeed lower in majoritarian systems. Our results, although strongly robust over samples and methods, do exhibit one obvious limitation: they only capture the two endpoints of a long process between incentives and outcomes. How specifically do legislators bring about higher prices when votes are valued less and the obverse when they are valued more?

Our theory posits that regulatory policy is the key. Where legislators privilege producers, they insulate them from competition through regulations such as licensing schemes or barriers to entry for new competitors. Where consumers are ascendant, liberalization rules the day. Our theory is consistent with our results – producer-coddling regulation should raise real prices – but it is possibly not the only theory to connect electoral arrangements to price levels. Might other regularities between proportional and majoritarian countries explain price differences? Without a closer empirical examination of the mechanism, the actual policy-forming behavior of legislators under different electoral regimes, we cannot rule out rival explanations. We address these concerns here.

This chapter differs from its predecessors in both method and substance. Chapter 2 built a formal theoretical framework; Chapters 3 and 4 have presented systematic and copious empirical evidence; this chapter now reduces the level of abstraction with a concrete case study and the explicit empirical examination of our mechanism. While case studies cannot prove any relationship – perhaps even less so than other methods – they offer a valuable tool to illustrate how a model corresponds to actual events. In so doing, they strengthen theory by showing plausibility and highlighting possible mechanisms. Let us, however, also be explicit about what cannot be achieved: with the exception of some rare natural experiments in which nothing but the key independent variable changes, case studies cannot identify which variables precipitate an outcome, simply because they cannot control for simultaneous variation in multiple potentially causal variables. Indeed, because they only consider a single observation, they also cannot rule out causal processes that are absent in this specific case. There is no way to know whether the observed case is an outlier from a larger pattern. So why offer a case study? It offers insight into the complexity of the policy-making process and how outcomes may come about. With these caveats in mind, this chapter is devoted to an empirical examination of how electoral incentives influence or at least antecede regulatory outcomes and, consequently, prices.

We begin with a brief and simple comparison of regulatory policies across electoral systems. Politicians have a large and complex palette of policy tools by which they can insulate favored producer interests from competition. This abundance of policy tools obviously complicates the comparison of pro-producer regulation across countries because differences can emerge in various, sometimes unmeasured, policy areas. In general, we argue that this makes the ultimate outcome of all constraints on competition – higher prices – the best measure of systematic regulatory differences between countries. As our purpose here, however, is to expose the mechanism, we first examine a common means of privileging producers: barriers to entry for new competitors. At the same time, our case studies – in particular, that of Italy – will underline the point that electoral systems are ultimately endogenous, with informed producers (especially monopolists) strongly favoring proportional methods of election.

Next, we turn to a promising natural experiment. The early 1990s saw an unusual number of shifts in electoral law in developed countries with Italy and Japan abandoning mostly proportional systems (single nontransferable vote, or SNTV, in the case of Japan) for mixed systems in which the preponderance of seats was chosen from single-member districts (three-quarters of the seats in Italy, two-thirds in Japan). In 1993, New Zealand switched in the opposite direction from what had often been regarded as the world's purest Westminster system, bar none (unicameral parliamentary system; two major parties; single-member districts) to a proportional system with majoritarian trappings (mixed-member proportional, essentially copied from Germany). Each of these countries offers a rare opportunity to examine the changes in economic regulation that followed the introduction of a new electoral system. We focus here on Italy, but suspect that Japan and New Zealand would offer equally illuminating reforms.

In the closing section of the chapter, we then turn to two countries that experienced large shifts in their level of electoral competitiveness and again study changes in regulation and price levels. The mechanism of our argument, the different seats-votes elasticities under SMD and PR that yield different policy-making incentives for lawmakers, is effectively a proxy for electoral competition. Where small shifts in vote share correspond to large swings in seat share (SMD), competition is high and votes are dear; where vote share equals seat share (PR) or where shifts in vote share correspond to very little change in seat share (SMD in an uncompetitive, particularly a single-party dominant system), votes matter relatively less and money relatively more. What the seats-votes elasticity (τ) captures is essentially electoral competitiveness, or at least an important component thereof. Thus we should expect large changes in electoral competitiveness to manifest themselves in regulatory and price shifts much as would a change in electoral system. Legislators should be less inclined to enact competition-reducing regulations to protect producers when electoral competition is strong.[1] We test this argument on two countries that have experienced large shifts in electoral competitiveness, the United States and India.

Competition-Reducing Regulation across Electoral Systems

The assertion that governmental regulation can and often does serve the interests of the regulated is certainly not new. Arguments about the "capture" of regulatory agencies by producers were already made famous by the early successes of the public choice school of Buchanan, Tullock, Stigler, Peltzman, and others. Their argument contrasted sharply with the then predominant view of regulation as a means of countering negative externalities, monopoly competition, and other

---

[1] Although we do not wade into electoral behavior, our logic here builds on John Zaller's argument that real disposable income (RDI) is the best predictor of the incumbent vote share (in the United States). Higher prices, by definition, lower real income and, per Zaller, lower incumbent vote share as well.

139

market failures (see, for example, Pigou 1938). A cottage industry of empirical and theoretical work has emerged around this debate but it is only more recently that scholars have begun to examine how political institutions structure regulatory incentives and outcomes.

The influential research of Djankov et al. (2002) first showed that regulation in a key area for the welfare of established producers – the entry of new competitors into existing markets – responds to institutional incentives. Regulators inhibit the entry of new firms more where democracy is weak and government expansive. Consistent with the public choice theory of regulation, they find that this heavy hand of government in regulating entry is associated with greater levels of corruption and more extensive unofficial economies, but not with greater quality of public or private goods. While their measures are ones of democracy – constraints on executive power, *de facto* executive independence, the effectiveness of the legislature, competition in the legislative nominating process, and the Polity III Autocracy score – it is important to note that what Djankov et al. ultimately find is the effect of **political competition**. Consequently, it should not be entirely surprising that other institutions that mediate political competitiveness also influence regulatory behavior – and ultimately, we argue, real price levels.

Scartiscini (2002) confirmed the regulatory effect of electoral systems. Proportional, as opposed to majoritarian, electoral systems have been associated with more extensive welfare systems, greater budget deficits (Persson and Tabellini 2003), higher government spending (Milesi-Ferretti, Perotti, and Rostagno 2002), and more frequent strikes (Vernby 2007). Scartiscini, however, argued that the way in which legislators (and their agents) respond to organized and unorganized interests had consequences for which groups are privileged under SMD and PR. Following Bawn and Thies' (2003) modification of Denzau and Munger's (1986) model, Scartiscini demonstrated empirically that majoritarian electoral systems yield significantly lower barriers to entry than their proportional counterparts.

More precisely, Scartiscini investigates how electoral arrangements influence the four specific barriers to starting and operating a new business first examined by Djankov et al.: the number of procedures, the number of days for licenses and approvals, cost, and cost plus time. Controlling for corruption (which, interestingly, reduces barriers to entry) and per capita GDP, he finds that majoritarian electoral systems are uniformly significant and negative predictors of entry regulation. This relationship, estimated from a sample of sixty-five democracies around the world, holds for the proportion of single-member-district seats in the legislature, a plurality dummy, and a form of inverted district magnitude (the number of districts divided by the number of directly elected legislators). This result – which contrasts with weak results for other institutional features such as presidentialism, federalism, bicameralism, and particularism – also speaks to the primacy of the electoral system in influencing electoral strategy and, consequently, regulatory behavior.

Hewing to the implicit theme of this chapter that simpler is sometimes better, we plot the distribution of the four barriers to entry employed by Djankov et al. in Figure 5.1.[2,3] Even in a small, twenty-three-country OECD sample, without controls for corruption or income, a difference between systems emerges.[4] By all four measures, the mean barrier to entry is lower in SMD states. The difference in the number of procedures and the cost of starting and operating a new business is trivial. The difference in the mean number of days required to complete all procedures, however, is quite substantial – nine

---

[2] Data are from 1999 and are available at http://www.doingbusiness.org/ExploreTopics/StartingBusiness/.

[3] Djankov et al. made several assumptions about the data to ensure comparability across countries. The business is (1) a limited liability company, (2) operates in the country's most populous city, (3) is completely owned domestically and has at least five owners, (4) has start-up capital of ten times income per capita, (5) performs general industrial or commercial activities but no foreign trade activities, (6) leases space and is not a proprietor of real estate, (7) does not qualify for investment incentives or any special benefits, (8) has at least ten and up to fifty employees one month after commencement of operations, all of them nationals, (9) has a turnover of at least 100 times income per capita, and (10) has a company deed at least ten pages long.

[4] The countries sampled are: Australia, Austria, Belgium, Canada, Denmark, Finland, France, Germany, Greece, Iceland, Ireland, Italy, Japan, Luxembourg, Netherlands, New Zealand, Norway, Portugal, Spain, Sweden, Switzerland, United Kingdom, and the United States.

Barriers to Starting and Operating a New Business, OECD23

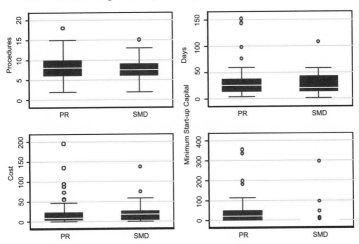

Figure 5.1. Electoral system and competition-reducing regulation

in SMD, sixteen in PR – and the minimum start-up capital shows a large and statistically significant gap. On average, entrepreneurs in majoritarian member states of the OECD23 need deposit only 7 percent of mean per capita GDP to start a company, while their counterparts in PR states faced a barrier of 16 percent. Logging these variables to reduce the influence of outliers does little to change the results.

These findings, of course, are more illustrative than definitive. We refer readers interested in more rigorous investigation to Djankov et al. (2002) and Scartiscini (2003).[5] Our

---

[5] Rosenbluth and Schaap (2003) also offer corroboration from the banking industry: Centripetal electoral systems (roughly: SMD) force banks rather

purpose here is primarily to examine first a static cross-sectional relationship in order to inform our case study in the following section. If countries with majoritarian electoral arrangements exhibit less competition-reducing regulation of business – and, consequently, lower real prices – should not changes in electoral system also imply changes in regulation and prices? We turn to Italy's experiment with majoritarianism to answer this question.

A Natural Experiment: Electoral Laws, Competition, and Regulatory Reform in Italy, 1993–2005

Long an epitome of proportionalism – perhaps of its flaws more than its advantages – Italy radically reformed its electoral system in the early 1990s to a mixed-member majoritarian system in which three-fourths of parliamentary seats were allocated to single-member district elections and the remaining one-quarter continued to be filled through list PR. Changes of electoral system have been extremely rare in developed countries since World War II, so examining even one case in detail offers important insights. If the cross-sectional association between electoral systems and regulation is indeed causal, we would expect a similar pattern to

than banking customers to pay for the stability of the financial system while the obverse holds under centrifugal (roughly: PR) electoral systems.

emerge over time as well. Italy's change of electoral system offers a rare opportunity (1) to see whether changes in electoral arrangements precede changes in regulation and (2) to examine the particular process by which regulatory reform occurs in greater detail.

In the remainder of this section, we examine origin and implementation of Italian regulatory reform in considerable detail. Our theory predicts a shift toward economic liberalization under the electoral incentives of Italy's experiment with majoritarianism. The multiple origins of regulatory policy and sometimes conflicting effects of numerous variables other than electoral incentives, of course, ensure a complex path to the rollback of anticompetitive regulations. We nevertheless conclude that the introduction of a predominantly majoritarian electoral system between 1993 and 2006 was both a tool for and a source of Italian regulatory liberalization.

The Demand for Economic Reform

As with most social and economic phenomena, multiple factors contributed to regulatory reforms in the Italian economy. Prominent on this list was the weakening economic performance that Italy experienced in the late 1980s and 1990s. The OECD (2002) estimates that potential (i.e., full employment) GDP growth in Italy experienced the largest decrease of all major European economies between the 1980s and 1990s. In per capita GDP growth, the Italian economy sank to a middle ranking among European economies after consistently ranking near the top during the 1980s. Simple conditional convergence – diminishing marginal returns on investment in a constant returns model – explains some of this slowdown. Italian output per capita simply caught up with that of its neighbors (Barro and Sala-i-Martin, 1995). Declining growth in multifactor productivity (MFP) – essentially a multiplier on factor inputs into an economy – also explains some of this change. In a study of growth rates in the OECD (2001c), the OECD explains this drop in MFP growth as a consequence of limited usage of information and communications technology and low spending on research and development but, notably, also as a result of weak competition in product markets.

The need to reform the regulation of Italian product markets to spark innovation and competition was widely understood in the early 1990s. Politicians and businesspeople alike recognized the importance of raising domestic competitiveness given the expected competition both from the Single European Act (SEA), which removed barriers to trade for goods within the European Union in 1992 and from the European Economic and Monetary Union (EMU) that Italy aspired to join at the end of the decade. For decades, Italy had avoided reforms to competition policy and the labor market (among other areas), through a combination of protectionist barriers, collusion of producers and, when unavoidable, currency devaluation to lower real prices and thus boost international competitiveness. This represented a systematic privileging of producer over consumer interests as competition from foreign producers and among domestic producers would have lowered real prices without devaluation. Repeated devaluations, similarly, eroded the real incomes and domestic savings of consumers. The SEA and EMU required that Italy find a new means of maintaining international competitiveness: domestic reform. Nevertheless, Italy, wracked with patronage and corruption, proved incapable of reform in the first half of the 1990s. Vincenzo Visco, a former finance minister, captured the frustration of the period: "Italy appeared to be, and indeed was, a country without an economic discipline, characterized by a low level of social cohesion, mal-governed by a ruling class that was incapable of making brave choices, that yielded to the requests and pressures exercised by interest groups, and which was increasingly and openly corrupt and therefore less authoritative."

Italian bureaucracy for most of the postwar years was burdensome, inefficient, and corrupt. Between the 1950s and 1990s, the Italian state erected an increasingly interventionist web of regulatory requirements, procedures, and rules. Italian legislation – regulatory or otherwise – rarely repealed earlier legislation so, in effect, the state successively laid down layers of confusing, anticompetitive, and sometimes contradictory demands. The public administration could not fully implement much of the legislation, nor could even the most punctilious members of the public comply. The accumulation of regulations together with their low quality – sometimes only social statements of preference, devoid of all details, legislated for political purposes – generated complexity and ambiguity. As a consequence, much regulation became a negotiation between regulators and the regulated, inviting corruption and undermining accountability. Interest groups often captured portions of the administrative bureaucracy that allowed them, in turn, to form policies favorable to incumbent producers and against those of potential market competitors.[6]

In many countries, blaming corruption for political outcomes (or the lack of reform) is little more than populist rhetoric; in Italian politics, however, corruption is indeed an important explanatory variable. Examining judicial requests for the removal of legislator's immunity, Chang, Golden, and Hill (2007) report that an astounding 54 percent of all deputies who served in the Italian lower house between 1948 and 1994 were charged with criminal wrongdoing. Many of these charges were minor and politically motivated, but even the proportion charged with major crimes – quite often involving accusations of political corruption, illegal party financing,

---

[6] Many of the characterizations and assertions of this paragraph find support in OECD's (2001b) *Regulatory Reform in Italy.*

or abuse of office – remains impressively high: the median proportion of deputies charged with major crimes in the eleven postwar legislatures before 1994 was slightly more than 15 percent, while the final legislature elected under PR reached the dubious landmark of 35 percent of deputies charged with serious malfeasance. In 1995, Italy ranked 32 out of 41 countries in the Transparency International corruption index, a remarkable achievement for an advanced industrial country.

The chronic inability of the Italian legislature to reform itself or the economy and its insulation from voters and consumers was likely related to the low levels of political accountability. Consistent with the conventional understanding that PR delivers less accountability (Powell 2000) and, consequently, greater corruption (Kunicova and Rose-Ackerman 2005, Tavits 2007) than majoritarian systems, Chang, Golden, and Hill (2007) report that the only legislature in which accusations of serious criminal wrongdoing hurt deputies' probability of reelection was the eleventh and final one that faced reelection during the collapse of the Italian party system. Little reform, regulatory or otherwise, took place under the proportional arrangements that governed Italian elections for most of the postwar period.

Italian voters became increasingly frustrated with the absence of economic and political reform. Just as increasing exposure to international economic competition under the terms of the SEA raised demand for greater competitiveness in the early 1990s, the *mani pulite* (clean hands) judicial investigations of the early 1990s, which revealed widespread corruption among public officials at even the highest levels, increased the public demand for political change. This came to a head in April 1993, following a stream of corruption accusations against prominent officials including even Bettino Craxi, leader of the Italian Socialist Party. Voters overwhelmingly backed a referendum that abolished Italy's proportional electoral system. It was replaced that August by a mixed-member majoritarian system.

Given the degree of corruption and deadlock in the Italian legislature, it is not surprising that the impetus for change in the electoral system came from outside of government and parliament. The Italian constitution, somewhat fortuitously, allowed an "abrogative referendum" by which voters, acting directly, could remove parts of legislation with which they disagreed. As Richard Katz (2006) reports, by removing thirteen words from the existing electoral law of the Senate, voters were able to convert a PR system into a mixed-system in which three-fourths of the members would be elected by plurality from single-member districts. Once the Senate's electoral arrangements were changed in the referendum of April 18, 1993, pressure mounted on the lower house of parliament to reform as well. The following August, after considerable dissent within the chamber, they adopted the Senate's new electoral system as their own.[7] This concession was too late to deflect the public's disillusionment, however, and voters again expressed their anger in the elections of March 1994, which ended the eleventh legislature and severely punished all of the governing parties elected in 1992. Eventually all four parties in the then-ruling coalition – the Christian Democrats, the Socialists, the Social Democrats, and the Liberals – would cease to exist, in a major realignment of the Italian party system. Ironically, the first government elected under SMD was that of Silvio Berlusconi in 1994, a prime minister certainly not associated, then or now, with reformist zeal against corruption or cosseted producers.

Electoral System Change as a Tool for Reform

In Chapter 2 of this book we described how electoral incentives under majoritarian electoral arrangements favor regulation that enhances competition and benefits consumers. This association of single-member-district systems with regulatory liberalization and reform, however, might also explain why reform-oriented actors have sometimes urged the abandonment of proportionalism. Thus, Italy's change of electoral system in 1993 might have been a tool for actors seeking

---

[7] Because the Italian constitution (Article 94) makes the cabinet equally responsible to both houses of parliament, it has long seemed essential to elect both by the same method.

to reform, among other things, the economic role of the state. Although it is certainly not necessary that politicians understand all the consequences of electoral system choice – indeed, many politicians probably remain ignorant of the existence, let alone the effects, of alternative electoral arrangements – it certainly is illustrative that in Italy in 1993 some politicians seemed aware of the link between SMD and pro-competitive policies.[8]

In Italy, the proposal for a predominantly majoritarian system – at first, only for the Senate – was placed on the referendum ballot by its chief advocates, the Committee for Democratic Reform (CORID), as one part of a package of measures intended to reduce sharply state intervention in the economy. Among the companion measures to the Senate electoral reform were (Donovan 1995, 56) abolition of:

- the Ministry for State Participation, which supervised parastatal corporations and hence controlled vast patronage;
- the Ministry of Agriculture, font of farmer-coddling subsidies and of rural patronage;
- partisan control over bank directorships.

---

[8] The other cases of electoral system change in our sample (France, Japan, and New Zealand) were either instigated for short-term strategic advantage (France) or offer too complex a transition to claim that awareness of implications for competition policy played a role (Japan, New Zealand).

A Closer Look: Case Studies and Mechanisms

While the major issue was undoubtedly Italy's unraveling web of corruption, nepotism, and thuggery, clearly the cartelistic structure of the economy, extensive subsidies, and out-of-control budgetary deficits were also important targets of the electoral reformers (ibid.). Only by abolishing the dominant "cartel" of parties, it was argued, could Italy's equally cartelized economy be freed from subsidies and state intervention (ibid. 50). Making these issues more urgent was the increasing competition to which the Italian economy was being opened, both by more fluid international financial markets and by its financial integration with the rest of Europe under the Single European Market, effective in 1992 (Golden 2004; Hiwatari 2001b, 4–6 and 14; Donovan 1995, 56). Moreover, the militantly pro-reform Northern League, which attacked particularly the subventions to Italy's South but emerged as a more general advocate of the North's economic vibrancy, moved swiftly (if somewhat opportunistically) to support the majoritarian system that it had initially opposed. Among electoral reform's leading opponents were the "cartel parties" – a majority of the Christian Democrats (DC), Craxi's Socialists (PSI), the Southern-anchored neo-Fascist Italian Social Movement (MSI), and (through its opposition to the leading reformer within the DC, Segni) the Catholic hierarchy (Donovan 1995, 54 and 58).

While it is a truism that many profound institutional changes are enacted by "sleepwalking" actors, unaware of deeper causes, in this instance some of the most important players seem to have understood, however imperfectly, the links among electoral system, economic competitiveness, and price levels.

The First Wave of Reforms, 1990–2001

The importance of the reforms that precipitated, accompanied, and resulted from Italy's switch to a predominantly majoritarian system cannot be overemphasized. Despite that two attempts at a "root-and-branch" reform of the Italian constitution failed – that of the D'Alema Bicameral Commission in 1998 and the center-right coalition's proposed constitutional amendments, rejected by the voters in 2006 – the legal and administrative reforms that did take place were unprecedented in the history of the Italian republic. The OECD (2001b) simply characterizes the changes of the early 1990s as "the most important reform of the Italian state since 1860." Legislators, likely mindful of their greater accountability for voters' welfare under majoritarianism, launched numerous initiatives under a succession of six governments. Competition-enhancing – and, hence, pro-consumer – policies were launched (1) to reduce the state's role in the economy through privatization, replacing old regulatory regimes and institutions and making laws and regulations both simpler and more transparent, (2) to limit the size of the public spending and borrowing (with an eye on EMU admissions requirements), and (3) to shift legislative, regulatory, and administrative authority to subnational levels of government. Government spending and regulatory giveaways would be constrained by a greatly strengthened finance ministry (Hallerberg, 2004, ch. 7).

In broad terms, these reforms succeeded. In the assessment of the OECD (2001b):

> The Italy of 2001 is far different from the Italy of 1990. Step by step, the interventionist producer-oriented, rigid and centralized state of postwar years is being transformed into a market-based, consumer-oriented, and decentralized state. This is being done through a continuing program of privatization, market liberalization and opening, deregulation followed by re-regulation, institution building, and regulatory quality initiatives.

Reform began with the enactment in 1990, even before the advent of the new electoral system and the Single European Market, of a competition law that enjoyed surprisingly effective enforcement throughout the decade. Then in 1993, among the other urgent reforms of that year, parliament passed legislation dramatically simplifying and restructuring regulatory and administrative bodies. The number of inter-ministerial committees was substantially reduced, independent authorities for public services – more insulated from politicians – were established, and new internal controls and audits of results were imposed on administrators (OECD 2001b). The election of the first government under the new three-quarters SMD electoral system in 1994, ironically delayed reform by sweeping into power, along with the new prime minister, Silvio Berlusconi, a class of officials who were provincial, inexperienced, and uninterested in international economic commitments (Visco 2002). The power of voters to hold the government accountable for economic discontent under the new electoral system, however, was soon demonstrated as economic crisis returned the Left (under Lamberto Dini) and accompanying fiscal reforms back to power the following year.

While the initial surge in reforms after 1993 focused most heavily on fiscal governance, by the second half of the decade legislators in the newly majoritarian parliament shifted focus to increasing competitiveness by reducing the state's intervention in the economy, privatizing enterprises, and opening markets. Italian privatization quickly became one of the largest programs among developed economies (OECD 1999b). Between 1996 and 2001, privatizations valued at a total of more than 82 billion Euros were completed (Visco 2002). As one consequence, stocks traded on the Italian Exchange increased by 400 percent in value, growing from a capitalization of some 10 percent of GDP in the early 1990s, to 70 percent in the spring of 2001, similar to that of

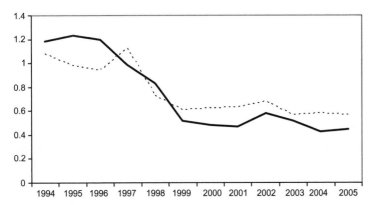

Figure 5.2. Total sectoral and ad hoc state aid as a percentage of GDP (Italy bold; EU15 dotted). *Source:* EuroStat: http://epp.eurostat.ec .europa.eu/portal/.

other European countries (ibid.).[9] An expanded private sector also called for better corporate governance – increasing transparency, protecting minority investors, and ensuring competition – which soon followed. In short, legislators, acting under predominantly majoritarian electoral incentives, removed the state from many of the economic sectors in which it had been deeply involved since the 1950s. State aid as a percentage of GDP only captures part of state involvement in the economy but EuroStat data in Figure 5.2 are indicative of the size of the change in the Italian economy in this period. Although European governments were, on average, retreating from direct

---

[9] In 1997 and 1998, in the rush to meet Maastricht requirements for entry into EMU, Italian privatization reached 2.4 and 1.1 percent of GDP, well above the European average (Vassallo 2007, 704).

involvement in the economy in the 1990s, changes in Italy outstripped those of its peers.

Not only did Italian legislators and their agents in the bureaucracy scale back state aid in the economy and privatize many state-owned enterprises, but they also dramatically restructured Italian regulation within a few years of the switch to SMD. A series of reforms after 1997, often adopting OECD guidelines on best practices, replaced layers of regulations accumulated over the postwar decades. Regulatory reform began in 1997 with a shift to fiscal federalism intended to reduce regulatory burdens. All competencies not explicitly reserved for the state were transferred to subnational units (Law 59/1997). The following year, parliament simplified administrative provisions and implemented an annual "delegislation" law that would require future governments to suppress administrative procedures and abolish concessions that were judged to have higher costs than benefits (Law 127/1998, 191/1998; Keesings and OECD 2001b).

The push toward enhancing competition can be seen in reforms of the retail sector early in the same year. The government of Romano Prodi proposed to abolish many of the regulations that protected Italian shopkeepers from competition. Shops of less than 300 square meters would be allowed to open without a license; all shops would be permitted to conduct business at any time between 7 and 10 P.M. up to a maximum of thirteen hours per day; and stores would be allowed

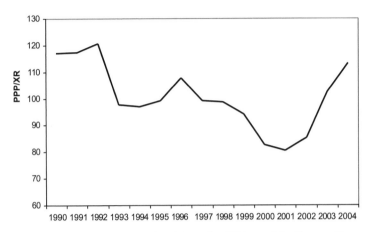

Figure 5.3. Real GDP price level in Italy (USA = 100). *Source:* Penn World Tables 6.2

to sell a greater diversity of products. Prior to these changes, regulations had insulated retailers from competition at the expense of higher price levels borne by consumers. Local outlets could only sell produce within one of fourteen narrowly defined categories. Grocers, for example, could not sell confectionery or tobacco, and butchers could not sell dairy products (Keesings).

Of course, such a large-scale shift in Italian regulation toward open competition and the interests of consumers should also be reflected in real price levels. Figure 5.3 reveals such a change. Italian real price levels, scaled against a level of 100 for the United States, experienced a precipitous drop after the advent of the Single European Market in 1992, then relative stability through the regulatory reforms of 1997, after which prices again steadily declined until the election of the second Berlusconi government in 2001. As we discuss later, however, the Berlusconi government marked a departure from the competition-enhancing reforms of the 1990s.

The final act in the string of pro-competitive reforms that followed Italy's shift to a more majoritarian electoral law arrived in 2001. The simplification bill of that year clarified, simplified, and reduced administrative hurdles to competition. It contained three important components. The *nucleo*, the relatively new unit of government responsible for administrative simplification, was given the right to submit proposals directly to the government, bypassing all ministries. The simplification bill also introduced the "guillotine system" to improve efficiency of regulatory codification. All of the rules to govern a particular sector would be laid down in new legislation and all preexisting rules in the sector would be annulled. Finally, opportunities for confusion and corruption were reduced by creating a centralized, electronic register of all administrative procedures and formats for business and forbidding administrators from requiring any formality not on the Web site. To gauge the scale of the push for deregulation, consider that approximately 10 percent of all legislative acts in the 13th and 14th legislatures (1996 to 2006) concerned deregulation provisions (Vassallo 2007, 701). Not all deregulation provisions, however, stimulated competition.

A Closer Look: Case Studies and Mechanisms

Competition Policy under Berlusconi, 2001–2005

The election of 2001 brought with it the return of Silvio Berlusconi to what would prove to be Italy's longest serving postwar government. The five years under the second Berlusconi government continued to see major institutional reforms but notably few reforms increasing market competition. Indeed, two of the most infamous reforms under Berlusconi consolidated the dominant market position of his media companies and inoculated him from prosecution for past business misdeeds.

The new government got off to an inauspicious start with its first reform: a "decree law" decriminalizing accounting fraud. Berlusconi himself was implicated at that time for offenses involving the establishment of slush funds by his own companies. Opposition politicians stated that among the hundreds of investigations dropped when accounting fraud was decriminalized were three charges against Berlusconi's business interests (Keesings, August 3, 2001). In 2004, parliament delegated the power to reform national broadcasting to the government. The reforms that emerged the following year reduced market competition by consolidating the dominance of the Prime Minister's own media group.

The momentum in government streamlining achieved in the late 1990s also tapered off. The consolidation of Italy's numerous governmental ministries promised to reduce uncertainty, redundancies, and contradiction in competencies and, of course, regulation. Although not the explicit purpose of governmental simplification, a smaller number of administrative bodies with clearer responsibilities would, in theory at least, reduce the bureaucratic hurdles imposed on business and increase competition. Here too, the Berlusconi government reversed direction. Following up on an earlier reform consolidating the Treasury, Budget, and Finance ministries, parliament passed a broader measure in 1999 reducing the number of Italian ministries – twenty-four in the 1980s, and still eighteen in 2001 – to twelve. By the time this came into force in 2001, however, the new center-right government had amended it to raise the number of ministries to fourteen, maintaining independent communications and health policy ministries (Vassalo 2007, 705).[10]

Reformers interested in improving Italian competitiveness were generally disappointed with the Berlusconi government. As expressed by Luca Cordero di Montezemolo, chairman of Fiat and Confindustria, the Italian business lobby, the highest priority for economic reform in Italy had been greater competition, which included privatization. Berlusconi, in Montezemolo's opinion, did not deliver (*Economist*, November 26, 2005). Possible evidence of this retreat from the

---

[10] The subsequent Prodi government again raised this number back to eighteen.

pro-competitive reform agenda of the 1990s can be seen in real price levels in Figure 5.3. In steady decline since the reforms of 1997, Italian real price levels, along with the balance of consumer-producer power, quickly reversed with the return of Berlusconi to power in 2001.

Though criticized for its failure to introduce competition to such industries as utilities, insurance, and financial services, as well as for limiting tax reforms to corporate taxes, the Berlusconi government did push through a cluster of three notable economic changes, all in 2003 and 2004. The government passed legislation raising the retirement age from fifty-seven to sixty in 2008 in order to cut pension expenditures. Parliament also approved the "Biagi Laws" liberalizing the labor market by, among other things, permitting for the first time jobs that were neither permanent nor full time.[11] Raising the retirement age and introducing flexibility into the Italian labor market, however, had little direct effect on the balance of consumer and producer interests. The final reform, however, did.

In 2004, one of Italy's largest companies, the food conglomerate Parmalat, was revealed to be bankrupt. As the accounting fraud that had allowed the company to amass large and unsupportable amounts of debt unfolded, analysts estimated

---

[11] Marco Biagi, the architect of the labor market reforms, was assassinated for his efforts.

that the cost to the Italian economy could amount to 1 per-cent of GDP (Keesings, January 2004). Resistance to financial sector reform quickly dissolved. By the end of the following year, parliament had returned the Bank of Italy, the primary financial regulatory body, to public ownership and transferred many of its regulatory powers to Italy's competition authority. Prior to the Parmalat scandal, the Bank of Italy, rather amaz-ingly, had been owned by a consortium of private banks and insurers which it, in turn, was responsible for regulating. It had long been reputed to protect domestic institutions from foreign banking competitors interested in the lucrative Ital-ian market – bank charges (and profits) were among the high-est in Europe (*Economist* 2005) – and had already come under scrutiny from the European Commission. (Keesings 2005).

In sum, although the Berlusconi government did shepherd through several reforms, its tenure represents a slowdown of reform, especially as regarded competition-enhancing (de)regulation. Most notably neglected was the service sector that, given the rising share of services in the Italian economy, as in most developed economies, was not negligible. In the last year of the Berlusconi government, services constituted about two-thirds of GDP (*Economist* 2005). Large swathes of the service sector were protected from competition through special rules and regulatory procedures. Small retail, taxis, pharmacies, notaries, and tradespeople were cited as espe-cially cosseted businesses in the press, but the single most important area was probably tourism. In 2005, the *Economist* noted that Italy's position as a tourist destination – top in 1970 – had fallen to fifth by 2005 because of underdevelopment and high prices – both likely the result of barriers to new competition.

The Carryover of Ongoing Reforms under the Left and PR: 2006 to the Present

One reform that the Berlusconi government had no compunctions about pushing through in the final months before its term expired was a return to proportional representation. Although it had been the largest beneficiary of the majoritarian reforms of 1993, the government did not hesitate to jettison majoritarianism when their waning popularity made an election under PR look less risky. In October 2005, the government pushed an electoral reform bill through both houses of parliament returning Italy to full PR before the 2006 elections, scheduled for April 9.[12] Surprisingly, perhaps partly because

[12] The Italian electoral law of 2005 has one majoritarian component built in to create stronger governing majorities. Parties form preelection coalitions. The coalition with a plurality of the national vote share (in the lower chamber) is then given bonus seats to raise them to 340 legislative seats (about 54 percent). In the Senate, the coalitions receiving a plurality of the vote in each region are awarded bonuses. The campaign against the 2005 electoral law argued that the Senate system was likely to result in unworkable majorities in the Senate or a hung chamber. The 2008 election dispelled this fear, however, rewarding a clear majority of 55 percent of the Senate seats to Silvio Berlusconi's coalition.

the backlash against the electoral changes, the Center-Right lost the April 2006 election. Romano Prodi came to power as prime minister at the head of a large and diverse coalition of centrist and leftist parties.

At first glance, the retreat from market competition under the Berlusconi government poses a challenge to our claim about majoritarianism. We assert, however, that few electoral incentives could overpower financial self-interest when the head of the government himself was one of the nation's preeminent producers; and it is indicative that, to try to insulate himself from consumer wrath, Berlusconi reinstated PR. All governments under SMD that did not have a direct material interest in suppressing competition, which is to say all except Berlusconi, presided over competition-enhancing reform. The three governments of the 13th legislature that immediately preceded Berlusconi, consistent with the pro-consumer electoral incentives of majoritarianism, enacted the single largest wave of pro-market reforms in postwar Italian history.

It would have been difficult to predict the tilt of regulatory policy after the second Berlusconi government ended in 2006. Unlike Berlusconi, Romano Prodi's government could be expected to respond to electoral rather than financial incentives; but at the time many elected officials expected a return to a mostly SMD electoral system before the next election. Indeed, when the government did fall in January 2008,

Giorgio Napolitano, the Italian president, did attempt, albeit in vain, to revise the election law before new elections.

Thus, the new government pressed ahead with delayed reforms of the service sector. Partly because of the Left's past criticism of Berluconi's failure to reform the service sector and because of uncertainty about how long the current PR rules would endure, and very likely because the small service providers who would be most affected tended to vote for the Center-Right, the Prodi government guided through legislation to improve consumer welfare. Taxi drivers, pharmacists, lawyers, veterinarians, notaries, banks, and bakers lost special protections from competition under a set of reforms named after the economic development minister Pierluigi Bersani.[13] The press reported estimates that the average Italian family would save approximately 1,000 Euros per year (*Economist* 2006a). In October of the same year, it passed competition-augmenting legislation for one more area protected under the previous government, the private television market in which Berlusconi's four channels exercised a near monopoly.

---

[13] Among other things, the "Bersani Decree" increased the number of taxi-licenses, allowed cabs to be driven by more than one license-holder, permitted local government to impose fixed fares for certain taxi routes, allowed nonprescription drugs to be sold outside of pharmacies as long as a pharmacist was present, abolished minimum fees for lawyers and veterinarians, legalized "no-win, no fee" payments for lawyers, and removed notary requirements for selling used vehicles.

Italy in Conclusion

The resurgence of liberalizing reforms after Italy's return to PR as well as the slackening of competition-enhancing reforms during the final five years of majoritarianism testifies to the complex collection of factors that motivated politicians to tilt policy toward consumers or producers. The facts that major reforms first emerged with the shift to SMD, and that SMD had been advocated precisely as a means to such reforms, suggests an important role for majoritarianism. The Berlusconi government's aversion to continued liberalization speaks to another determinant: the partisan orientation of the likely beneficiaries and losers. Berlusconi was hesitant to harm small business in the service sector, a core constituency for the center Right; but the Prodi government, once in power, did not hesitate. And it is revealing that Berlusconi, having repudiated reform, reenacted PR. Finally, no accounting of the causes of regulatory reform in Italy can neglect the dire economic need for more competitive firms able to compete in the single European market introduced in 1992 and the more responsible fiscal policy necessary to gain admission to the nascent European Economic and Monetary Union.

It is probably most accurate to describe the relationship between the electoral system and liberalizing reforms as mutually reinforcing. Reformers supported a shift to SMD because they associated it with the capacity for change.

168

A Closer Look: Case Studies and Mechanisms

Once SMD (MMM) was in place, it reinforced the direction of change as legislators realized the heightened value of votes under SMD. It is difficult to overestimate the degree to which four decades of single-party dominance under PR had entrenched anticompetitive regulations favoring special interests. In its survey of Italy in 2005, over a decade after the switch to majoritarianism, the *Economist* still described Italians as suffering from "a pervasive anti-business, anti-customer culture," and noted that "Italians may be entrepreneurial and creative, but they are by no means pro-market." That may be so, but no observer of Italian reform in the last two decades can deny that a remarkable shift toward liberalization and competitive markets has taken place.

Electoral Competitiveness and Consumer Power in the United States

Few countries ever change their electoral system, a fact that seems to preclude extensive case study. Although our mechanism focuses on how electoral systems change electoral incentives, the seats-votes elasticity in different electoral systems is but one component of electoral responsiveness. The electoral system governs how vote shares affect contestation in districts but, of course, the balance of vote shares itself should also affect incumbents' electoral incentives and regulatory behavior. In countries where the electoral system

169

has not changed, it is electoral competitiveness that matters for consumer power. In this final section, we examine how changes in political competiveness have affected the balance of consumer-producer power in the United States.

Consider first the argument: the different seats-votes elasticities that yield different policy-making incentives for lawmakers in different electoral systems are effectively a proxy for electoral competition. Where small shifts in vote share correspond to large swings in seat share (SMD), competition is high and votes are valued; where vote share equates to seat share (PR) or where shifts in vote share correspond to very little change in seat share (e.g., SMD with many "safe" seats), votes matter relatively less and money relatively more. The seats-votes elasticity (τ) captures the rate at which electoral shifts are translated into changes in seat share. Of course, this is only one facet of electoral competitiveness.[14] Our stripped-down model in Chapter 2 assumes an even split of electoral support between two parties, thereby isolating τ, the seats-votes elasticity, as the measure of electoral competitiveness that should influence legislators. Once parties' vote shares diverge, however, both τ and vote share should matter until we reach the opposite extreme.[15] When one party is highly dominant – for

[14] See Kayser and Linzer (2008) for a method of fully measuring electoral competitiveness across different electoral systems.

[15] We even showed in Chapter 2 that the consumer advantage of SMD should be surpassed by proportional systems in cases of extremely weak electoral competition.

example, Mexico under PRI, India under the Congress Party, or Japan in the heyday of the LDP – even a large τ is unlikely to affect the incentives of legislators.

Because the elasticities of SMD ($\tau \approx 2.5$) and PR ($\tau \approx 1$) systems are well known, cross-national research comparing majoritarian and proportional electoral systems offers a useful, if rough, tool to examine the broader effects of electoral competition in cross-national research. In a single-country case study where the electoral system does not change, electoral competitiveness itself is what matters. Absent changes to the electoral system, however, most countries rarely experience large shifts in electoral competition. One prominent exception – and the one we examine here – is the United States.

In the early 1970s, political scientists began to document a dramatic decline in the level of electoral competitiveness in elections for the U.S. House of Representatives. Robert Erikson (1972) revealed that incumbency advantage was increasing; Edward Tufte (1973) demonstrated that the swing ratio – the increase in seats associated with a given increase in the vote – was declining; and, most famously, David Mayhew (1974) showed that the average portion of the two-party vote captured by incumbents had risen while the number of competitive races has dropped. The number of competitive districts – those won by 10 percent of the two-party vote or less – in the U.S. House elections declined from an average of

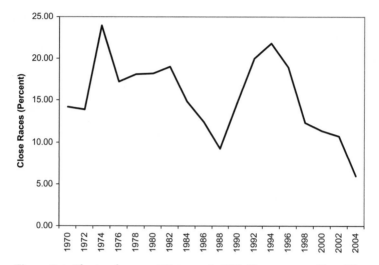

Figure 5.4. Electoral competitiveness in U.S. House races. *Note:* The *y*-axis represents the percentage of House races contested by both major parties in which the two-party vote margin was less than 10 percent. Notice spikes following the Watergate scandal and the 1994 Republican takeover of the House (Gingrich's Contract with America and the Southern realignment). Compiled by author from district level election results. Data sources: CQ Voting and Elections Collection, America Votes 26, 2004–2004 (Richard M. Scammon, ed.), and "United States Congressional Elections, 1788–1997," (Michael J. Dubin, ed).

ninety-four between 1956 and 1964 to only fifty-nine in 1972. Since Mayhew's observation, as we document in Figure 5.4, this trend has continued. Indeed, in the 2004 House elections the number of districts that qualified as competitive by Mayhew's definition sank to twenty-two.

A Closer Look: Case Studies and Mechanisms

The causes of this long-term decline in electoral competitiveness, rare for a developed democracy, are highly disputed. Scholars have advanced competing theories, locating the source of growing incumbency advantage in areas as diverse as a decline in partisan identification (Erikson 1972, Ferejohn 1977), name recognition and House franking privileges (Mayhew 1974), the growth of the bureaucracy (Fiorina 1977), incumbent quality (Zaller 1998), campaign finance (Green and Krasno 1988) and gerrymandering (Tufte 1973; Cox and Katz 2002).

More consensus prevails on the likely consequences of rising incumbency advantage. The growing weight that voters seem to give to incumbents rather than to their parties when casting their vote implies a decline in the effectiveness of parties and their responsiveness to voters. Among other effects, the growing personal vote suggests that congressional leaders have less influence over the rank-and-file (Collie and Brady 1985) and presidents less influence over congressional co-partisans (Edwards 1980). More worrisome are concerns about responsiveness to voters. Insulated incumbents, accustomed to lopsided victories and weak challengers, have weaker incentives to promote the interests of voters, diminishing the value of each vote and, we predict, tilting their regulatory priority toward consumers.

Against these claims stands a secondary literature asserting that electoral competitiveness, measured correctly, has not changed. Most prominently, Gary Jacobson (1987) has argued that greater volatility in the vote means that "incumbents are no safer now than they were in the 1950s; the marginals – properly defined – have not diminished, let alone vanished; the swing ratio has fallen little, if at all; and so competition for House seats held by incumbents has not, in fact, changed." Others have identified the vanishing marginals as a self-selection problem. After a series of landmark judicial rulings on congressional reapportionment in the 1960s,[16] the more frequent redrawing of constituency boundaries enabled incumbents in facing redistricting to anticipate a competitive race and retire (Cox and Katz 2002). These retirements, they argue, lowered the number of incumbents involved in close elections and increased the average advantage of those who remained.

Despite such skepticism, there is strong evidence that both electoral competitiveness and congressional responsiveness to votes have declined in the United States. As we discussed previously, two important components of electoral competitiveness are vote margins and the seats-votes relationship. As Ansolabehere, Brady, and Fiorina (1992) argue, the debate about the consequences of declining electoral competition has gone astray by focusing on the first while

---

[16] *Baker v. Carr,* 1962; *Gray v. Sanders,* 1963; *Reynolds v. Sims,* 1964; *Wesberry v. Sanders,* 1964.

the U.S. House has experienced a decline in the latter. It does seem that incumbents in "safe" districts are indeed less "safe" as Jacobson argued. Moreover, incumbents' response to greater uncertainty – more trips to their constituencies, more constituency service, and more resources for their districts – does suggest that the responsiveness of individual legislators to their constituents has not declined.[17] However, this is beside the point: What matters is whether the responsiveness of Congress as a whole has declined.

The decline in the number of marginal districts and the growth in the volatility of vote margins imply that "defeats of incumbents today are less systematic than in the 1950s." That is, a national shift in vote share implies less of a shift in seat share for a party than it did in earlier decades when marginal districts were both more numerous and more dangerous to incumbents than they are in the present. There are indeed fewer marginal districts, and incumbents in these districts are indeed less endangered than they used to be, even while colleagues in seemingly safer districts may be less safe. Thus the change in the distribution of vote margins itself has not insulated individual representatives who suddenly find themselves ensconced in 'safe' districts. The decline in the number of (and peril to incumbents in) marginal districts, however, has had large repercussions for parties as a

---

[17] See Griffin (2006) for an argument to the contrary.

whole by lowering, contrary to Jacobson's claim, the swing-ratio – akin to what we estimate as the seats-votes elasticity.[18] Ansolabehere, Brady, and Fiorina carefully document this decline and thereby explain the puzzling absence of a drop in the responsiveness of individual representatives – at least as measured by contact to their constituents.

We devote the remainder of this section to examining the consequences of this drop in the seats-votes ratio. As we argue throughout this book, any such change should bear consequences for the regulatory tilt of legislators toward consumers and producers. By examining the U.S. House of Representatives in detail, we have been able to establish with greater certainty a case in which electoral competitiveness dropped. Consistency with our theory, of course, demands that the regulatory advantage of producers over consumers should also diminish. As we argued earlier, the best way to measure such advantage – which can materialize in numerous highly varied forms – is through measuring the ultimate purpose of regulatory protection: changes in prices. When producer influence waxes, we expect concurrent increases in consumer prices. Of course, prices increases can also arise from international shocks to supply or demand, not just from changes in the

---

[18] There are many methods of measuring the "swing ratio," of which ours is only one.

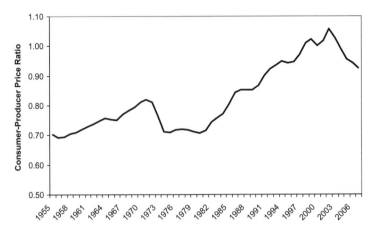

Figure 5.5. Producer Advantage. *Source:* OECD Main Economic Indicator Producer Price Index and Consumer Price Index series.

regulatory tilt of government. We accordingly employ here the ratio of consumer to producer prices as a measure of producer advantage.[19] Higher consumer prices relative to those paid by producers, of course, favor producers. Thus, we call this ratio "producer advantage."

Certainly, in no way does the broad co-movement of two trends establish causality, although as a necessary condition, it establishes plausibility. That is all we can hope for with such a simple analysis. As Figure 5.5 demonstrates, movements

---

[19] The indexed PPP/XR measure of real prices used in the earlier chapters is not an option for the United States because these data are indexed to a baseline value of 100 for the United States.

in U.S. price levels broadly comport with our argument that secure legislators favor narrow over broad interests. Much as legislators in countries with PR systems (low 'swing ratios') value votes and, hence the interests of consumers, less than do their counterparts in majoritarian systems (high 'swing ratios'), changes in the seats-votes relationship in the United States over time yield corresponding shifts in the power of consumers. The long decline in electoral competitiveness in the U.S. Congress – as captured in the declining number of seats captured by a given increase in a party's national vote share – has been associated with an attendant erosion of consumer power. This association, we argue, is no coincidence but attributable to the interests of rational representatives.

Conclusion

Chapters 3 and 4 of this book exposed a substantively strong and robust relationship between electoral arrangements and real price levels across countries and over time. This chapter has examined this relationship in greater detail – first in terms of barriers to entry, a key regulatory variable related to prices, then via a case study of the regulatory consequences of the change in the Italian electoral system, and finally via brief examination of the changes in electoral competitiveness in the United States. Following our theory developed in Chapter 2, we posited that different electoral incentives of legislators yield changes in regulation that systematically favor consumers or producers. Case studies certainly do not establish causality, nor do they perform well in assessing the relative magnitude of various causal variables. However, they do highlight plausible sources of causation, causal paths, and interactions. By examining actual cases of change in electoral system and electoral competitiveness, we now have greater confidence that regulatory change, with its price implications for consumers and producers, often follows changes in political incentives.

We have demonstrated that proportional systems are systematically, albeit not always significantly, associated with producer-friendly regulation – such as barriers to entry for new competition – that suppresses market competition and yields higher prices. We are now also more confident that legislators indeed respond to the electoral incentives in majoritarian systems by favoring consumer-friendly policies such as deregulation, administrative simplification, privatization, and removal of quotas that raise market competition and lower prices. Despite the noise inherent to any detailed study, our examination of a rare natural experiment – Italy's experimentation with majoritarianism between 1993 and 2006 – has shown that the single biggest wave of regulatory reform in Italian history began a few years after the adoption of a predominantly SMD system. Of no less interest is that several of the actors who initiated the electoral reform of 1993 were known advocates of liberalization, and that an antireform government returned to PR.

Our theory, of course, bears implications not only for cases of wholesale electoral system change but also for any nontrivial shift in electoral incentives. We therefore also predict and find price consequences from the decline of electoral competitiveness in the U.S. House of Representatives. In both Italy and in the United States, when votes mattered more, legislators delivered more consumer-friendly policies and lower prices. In sum, closer examination of individual cases provides important insight into the often complex regulatory mechanism underlying our cross-national studies in Chapters 3 and 4.

6

Socioeconomic Origins
of Electoral Systems

Introduction

The analyses presented in the previous chapters highlight our basic argument – SMD systems consistently yield lower real prices. This strong empirical regularity holds up not only in the advanced OECD countries, as shown in Chapter 3, but also in developing democracies, as shown in Chapter 4. In addition to empirical evidence amassed from the cross-national comparisons, the electoral system-to-prices link is further corroborated in our detailed study of the Italian case, where the shift toward a majoritarian system was followed by regulatory liberalization and a reduction of real prices.

As we elaborated in Chapter 2, PR systems' association with higher real prices by no means contradicts the emerging consensus in the political economy literature that PR systems also enhance socioeconomic equality. However, here we explore the seeming paradox more fully.

What does the "consensus" literature say? Many argue that proportional representation encourages more generous redistribution, a point we take up at greater length presently. More directly, Birchfield and Crepaz (1998) show that PR is systematically related to lower income inequalities because it allows wider access to the policy-making process and hence better represents the interests of the poor. In light of these findings, one might naturally wonder how, if PR systems also empower producers and raise consumer prices, they can still promote equality. At an even deeper level, one might ask why PR systems can continue as an equilibrium: Why do consumers not demand a change that will reduce prices?

As our theoretical discussion of PR's welfare effects near the end of Chapter 2 will (we hope) have made clear, greater social equality is exactly what we would expect, at least initially, from the pro-producer regulation that PR engenders. Usually, organized workers rapidly become the strongest element within the producer coalition, and among organized workers the most numerous segment is the lower skilled. As we have shown, wage compression – including a wage higher than marginal product for low-skill labor – almost always ensues precisely where pro-producer coalitions dominate. Owners and managers are compensated (and often more than compensated) by the higher prices their products command (above all in nontraded sectors) and, almost always, by unions' commitment to training schemes that make initially less-skilled workers more productive. The losers from such arrangements, as others (e.g., Rueda 2007) have emphasized, are the "outsiders": less organized workers, unorganized homemakers, temporary workers, pensioners, the long-term unemployed, and (almost always) immigrants.

To put it more concisely: pro-producer policies entail both a welfare loss (to society as a whole) and a transfer – from the unorganized to the organized. In the short to medium run, those who receive the transfers are more than compensated for their share of the loss to social welfare. When, however, the welfare losses mount – and when, particularly, they rise suddenly because of some exogenous shock (a transport revolution opens previously sheltered sectors to trade, new immigrants increase the ranks of the unorganized) – then opposition to the system as a whole will rise, and clever politicians will exploit their opportunity.

This leads us to another legitimate concern about our previous findings, namely our implicit assumption that electoral systems are exogenous. Indeed, with the exception of the previous chapter, we treat electoral systems as fixed and we access their effects on real prices empirically. Our exogeneity assumption seems reasonable and justified, because empirically electoral systems change only rarely. Among the advanced democracies, only a few countries (among them

France, Italy, Japan, and New Zealand) have experienced substantial changes in their electoral systems since the early postwar era. Indeed, as Lijphart (1994) forcefully puts it, electoral systems as institutions "...tend to be very stable and resist change."

Nevertheless, the exogeneity assumption inevitably privileges the consequences over the origins of electoral systems. More importantly, as we briefly discussed in the earlier chapter, the exogeneity assumption might limit us from understanding the full link between electoral systems and policy outcomes. While the previous chapters establish that PR systems consistently lead to higher prices and greater socioeconomic equality, it might well be the case, as we have just noted, that many, or even most, voters in societies characterized by higher prices levels and greater socioeconomic equality have an incentive to maintain PR systems. In this sense, electoral systems could be self-sustaining, and through the feedback loop, the price effect of electoral systems identified earlier can even be self-reinforcing.

This chapter addresses explicitly this possibility, and hence relaxes the assumption of exogeneity in electoral systems. Several points, however, warrant our discussion before proceeding. First, in terms of modeling strategy, ideally it would be better to keep the original modeling setup and expand it into a fully dynamic model to tease out the causal complexity between electoral systems and socioeconomic equality. Specifically, it would be desirable to go back to the Stigler-Peltzman model and try to model the parameter τ as a function of the prices parameter, p_c. This task, however, turns out to be far from straightforward.

Nonetheless, the solution we adopt here bears a close kinship to the earlier discussion. Our measures of electoral-system responsiveness ask, in essence, how policy reacts to *variation* in the position of the median voter. More precisely, in our original Stigler-Peltzman setup, the agents were producers and consumers, but the key mechanism lay in the "responsiveness" variable (τ), which captured how seats in the legislature, and hence the balance of consumer-producer power, was affected by variation in the position of the electorate.[1] To take our leading example, if in a two-party system Party A moves from 49 percent to 51 percent of the vote (i.e., the median voter moves from slightly toward B to slightly toward A), then Party A typically moves from 47.5 percent of the seats to 52.5 percent in an SMD system, but from 49 to 51 percent in a PR system. That greater responsiveness to shifts in the median voter is what produces a more pro-consumer policy (we say) under SMD. However, typically, at least over the medium run, the median voter does not shift around all that much. What we begin to look at in this

---

[1] In SMD systems, the median voter; in PR systems, of any shift between voting blocs (because the τ is by design uniform).

chapter is, over that medium run, how much the typical position of that median voter differs, in income and ideology,[2] from that of the mean voter. Put differently, we address now not variation but *central tendency*, that is, the longer-term average position of the median voter – and, more specifically, how social welfare changes when the distance between the longer-term positions of the mean voter and those of the median voter widen or diminish. In taking this approach, we build on the seminal redistribution model of Meltzer and Richard (1981) and relate the choice of electoral systems to the strategic consideration of the pivotal voter (see later discussion).

Second, we distinguish ourselves from the existing literature with our theoretical treatment. Some more recent studies have attempted to examine the determinants of electoral systems and to model explicitly the endogenous choice of electoral rules. The prevalent idea of this school is that the adoption of electoral institutions accords with political actors' strategic calculations. To a first approximation, the choice of electoral systems is modeled as a problem of constrained optimization, where political elites choose the electoral regimes that will maximize their chances of winning under the current contextual constraint (Bawn 1993; Boix

---

[2] We adopt here the Meltzer-Richard position, explicated we hope more clearly later, that relative income maps directly onto ideology.

1999; Benoit 2004). Despite the progressive accomplishments of this latter approach, it has not addressed directly the issue of why, empirically, electoral systems change so rarely.

Instead of a top-down approach, this chapter attempts to provide an alternative bottom-up perspective to account for change and persistence in electoral systems. We posit that PR (majoritarian) systems systematically lead to greater socioeconomic equality (inequality), and that increases in equality (inequality) in turn sustain PR (majoritarian) systems. In other words, a reciprocal causality connects PR (majoritarian) systems and socioeconomic equality (inequality), and this self-reinforcing cycle is sustained by a variety of political and economic forces. Importantly, the self-reinforcing cycle between electoral system and socioeconomic equality may provide a previously unnoticed reason for institutional stability.

To foreshadow our argument, this chapter unpacks and presents the self-reinforcing cycle between electoral system and inequality in a sequential way. To begin with, we build on the existing theoretical and empirical literature that points strongly to the conclusion that countries with PR systems exhibit greater socioeconomic equality. For instance, many argue that proportional representation (PR) systems lead to more generous redistribution, because politicians under PR systems are elected from multimember districts and hence have incentives to seek broader support from the general

187

population (Lizzeri and Persico 2001; Milesi-Ferretti et al. 2002; Persson and Tabellini 2000, 2003, 2004). In addition to the direct effect of PR on redistribution, PR leads to higher redistribution indirectly because it yields higher turnout (usually implying less loss of Left votes) and hence tilts the location of the median voter farther away from the mean voter (Flora and Heidenheimer 1981; von Beyme 1985; Tavits 2004).[3] Even if we hold the median voter at the same location, the result remains unchanged, because PR systems are associated with a higher probability of Center–Left governments and hence with more extensive redistribution (Powell 2002; Iversen and Soskice 2006). Meanwhile, PR systems, due to their lower seats-votes elasticity, are found to increase real prices in favor of producers and thus usually improve low-skill workers' welfare, at least to the extent that they are organized in strong unions, via higher wages (see again Chapter 2). Taken together, these forces jointly lead to greater income equality in a society.[4] Lastly, this high income equality, sustained by higher wages and generous welfare policies, in turn either gives rise to PR regimes or reinforces societal preferences in favor of existing PR systems and against any shift to majoritarianism. The other side of the logic applies to the

---

[3] Income is skewed to the right, so adding Left voters moves median more than mean.

[4] Alesina et al. (2001) have shown empirically that redistributive policy indeed leads to higher income equality.

case of majoritarian systems, where the electoral system and socioeconomic inequality mutually reinforce each other.

What causes changes in electoral systems then? We argue, as outlined earlier, that electoral reform results from strong exogenous shocks that fundamentally unsettle the existing self-sustaining equilibrium. As Rogowski and MacRae (2008) argue, exogenous shocks resulting from changes in production technology or factor endowments can significantly affect social and economic (in)equality. Importantly, where these exogenous shocks increase inequality, the initially more equal society has incentives to shift to a majoritarian system, because such a change diminishes the loss in utilitarian social welfare. By contrast, decreasing inequality creates incentives for the society to broaden political participation and adopt PR systems. Using a simultaneous equation model, we test our hypothesis against Carles Boix's data on twenty-two democracies in the early twentieth century and find strong supporting evidence.

Hence, this chapter develops a unifying framework that accounts for both the consequences and the origins of electoral systems. The self-reinforcing cycle proposed in this study provides a previously unnoticed account for institutional stability and significantly enriches our understanding of electoral systems' short-term effects and their long-term evolutional dynamics. In the next section, we develop our model and elaborate our theory about the formation and persistence of electoral systems. Then we derive a set of hypotheses. In Section 3, we make use of Boix's data on electoral systems and Vanhanen's data on equality and test our hypothesis empirically. We then contrast our finding with alternative explanations of the choice of electoral systems. The final section concludes.

Theory

The path diagram in Figure 6.1 provides a graphical summary of our theory of self-reinforcing electoral systems. This self-reinforcing cycle can be decomposed into two components: The first concerns equality as a consequence; the second, equality as a cause of the electoral system. To facilitate our discussion, we discuss the case of PR systems, and readers can infer the case of majoritarian systems by the same logic.

Equality as a Consequence of Electoral Systems

A wealth of evidence and models now suggests that PR leads to higher social equality and majoritarianism to greater inequality, via a variety of political and economic mechanisms. We discuss them next.

Direct Redistribution Effect: An emerging branch of research in political economy asks whether and how electoral

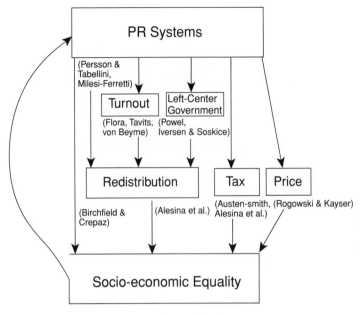

Figure 6.1. A theory of self-reinforcing electoral systems.

rules and other institutional arrangements (such as the division of power between the executive and the legislature, and between central and local government) shape the incentives of political actors and hence affect economic policy outcomes. PR systems are associated with societywide redistribution activities, whereas majoritarian/plurality systems are more likely to focus on district-specific spending on "pork." For instance, in a series of studies, Persson and Tabellini (2000, 2003, 2004) argue that multimember districts under PR systems encourage politicians to seek broader support in the population, whereas single-member districts under majoritarian/plurality systems instead concentrate electoral competition only in some geographical constituencies (i.e., those marginal districts with more swing voters). Because societywide redistribution programs, such as welfare and social security spending, are more effective in seeking broad support, and district-specic benets (i.e., "pork," loosely speaking) cultivate narrow support, they find that, compared to majoritarian systems, PR systems are characterized by higher redistributive spending.[5] One parallel redistribution effect induced by the difference between alternative electoral systems is that PR increases the size of the minimal winning coalition of voters needed by politicians. Under a stylized setting, a political party may need barely 25 percent of the national vote to win under a majoritarian system (i.e., slightly more than 50 percent of the vote in slightly more than 50 percent of the districts), while it needs 50 percent under PR. Politicians thus have stronger incentives to choose policy programs with societywide benefits under PR.

---

[5] Note that according to the model proposed by Persson and Tabellini (2000), parties under both PR and majoritarian systems will appeal and redistribute to the same group of voters; that is, the ones who are the least ideologically biased. Also, note that the rate of marginal votes gained from those ideologically neutral voters due to such redistribution is identical under both systems. What makes PR redistribute more is that the costs are smaller, because parties under PR do not internalize the votes lost from their core supporters.

Socioeconomic Origins of Electoral Systems

The finding that PR systems redistribute more than majoritarian ones is echoed in other studies. Unlike Persson and Tabellini, who rely on a preelection model where electoral platforms are binding, Milesi-Ferretti et al. (2002) construct a postelection model where policy is a product of bargaining among elected legislators. Milesi-Ferretti et al. further differentiate two types of spending: redistributive transfers, which go to anyone who meets the qualification criteria, and spending on goods and services that are locally targeted. According to their model, spending on transfers is higher under PR systems. This is because, under PR systems, more than one social group will be represented in the legislature. In such a situation, groups belonging to the ruling coalition derive their utilities from transfer spending (not on public goods and services, because those are uniform across groups). Hence, the median voter will bias the fiscal policy in his or her favor by selecting a legislator with a preference for high spending on transfers.

Indirect Redistribution Effect. PR has also been found to lead to more redistribution indirectly. Voter turnout is the first channel. As Tavits (2004) succinctly documents, turnout is higher under PR around the world, perhaps because of the normative appeal that PR is fairer or for the practical reason that PR provides more options for voters. (Even likelier, in our view, PR lacks the safe districts of majoritarian systems, in which parties have little incentive to mobilize voters, and voters little reason – knowing the outcome in their district is virtually pre-determined – to bear the costs of voting.) Importantly, poorer citizens also vote more frequently under PR, giving them more representation and power in political processes and forcing the government to be more responsive to their redistributive demands. This argument is consistent with Alesina et al.'s (2001) explanation of why European countries spend more on welfare than the United States, and is also in accordance with Powell (2000)'s finding that PR systems consistently bring governments' policies closer to the ideal position of the median voter, while majoritarian systems yield policies normally to the right of (i.e., less distributive than) the median voter. In addition, the higher turnout under PR pushes the location of the median voter toward the left (i.e., more redistributive) end of the ideological spectrum.

Another indirect path by which PR leads to higher redistribution is through the partisan composition of governments. Particularly, Iversen and Soskice (2006) argue that PR systems redistribute more than majoritarian ones because PR is likelier, holding the position of the median voter constant, to produce Center–Left governments. Their result is the optimal solution of the median voter after he or she conducts a cost-benefit analysis across all possible government coalitions. Specifically, under majoritarian systems, the Center–Right party is the lesser evil, because the worst-case scenario under a Center–Right government is no gain in the median voter's utility, while she can suffer utility loss under a Center–Left coalition because of the redistributive demands of the Left. By contrast, under PR systems, the median voter can vote for a median party that can ally with the Left (thus forming a Center–Left coalition government). The median voter is comfortable with this arrangement because its party can rein in any attempt by the Left to tax the middle class. In a similar vein, Powell (2002, esp. table 3) shows empirically that PR is associated with a higher frequency of Center–Left governments.

Tax Effect: Several studies have noted that PR countries typically exhibit higher tax rates and flatter post-tax income distributions (Alesina et al. 2001). To disentangle this empirical regularity, Austen-Smith (2000) develops a model of income inequality as a function of the tax system. He captures the trade-off between economic output (which is determined by the voters' endogenous choice of occupation) and distribution by assuming a labor-leisure tradeoff among individual voters who have different endowments of ability. He also assumes that parties are ideological and class (occupation) based. In equilibrium, PR systems have higher tax and unemployment rates, lower national incomes, and flatter post-tax income distributions, provided that the cost of choosing to work is relative low. Intuitively, the different electoral systems produce different sets of pivotal voters, who have different policy preferences: under majoritarian systems, the pivotal voter is the one with median income in the whole population, whereas under PR the pivotal voter is the one with average worker income, who may or may not be the same median individual identified under majoritarian systems. In addition, what drives a higher tax rate under PR is the two-edged effect from an increase in the tax rate: such an increase lowers net consumption utility but raises the income of the average employee by reshuffling the distribution of occupational choices. Therefore, as long as the cost of entering the workforce is low, a higher tax is preferred under PR because the income-increasing effect dominates the consumption-reducing effect, and this result holds regardless of whether electoral platforms are assumed to be binding.

Price Effect: In the previous chapters, we extended the Rogowski and Kayser (2002) argument that PR systems systematically privilege producers relative to consumers and, consequently, increase real prices. Our model considers a basic conflict between consumers and producers, the former seeking the lowest possible prices, the latter the highest possible prices consistent with profit-maximizing. Note that "producers" in our model explicitly include organized workers, who can more easily demand above-market wages when their industries enjoy above-market prices. Government can award producers the higher prices they seek, usually by restricting supply. Importantly, in deciding how much to restrict supply, politicians implicitly measure the marginal rate of substitution (MRS) between consumer and producer support: Where even a slight decrease in consumer support would require a large increase in producer support to keep a politician's overall level of support unchanged, consumers are powerful (and prices will be low); where a slight decrease in producer support must be offset by a large increase in consumer support, producers are powerful (and prices will be high). In Chapter 2, we show formally that any institutional change that increases the marginal value of votes must move the MRS in a more pro-consumer (hence, lower-price) direction. Because PR systems normally reduce the marginal value of votes, or more precisely lower the seats-votes elasticity, PR systems should be more pro-producer. Therefore, under PR systems politicians tilt their regulatory decisions toward restrictive supply and hence higher prices and (normally) higher wages for workers. We have presented supporting evidence in the previous chapters, both statistically, using OECD (Chapter 3) and world (Chapter 4) panels, and in historical case studies (Chapter 5).

In sum, several derivations from the existing theoretical and empirical literature all lead to the same implication: Countries with PR (majoritarian) systems are associated with greater socioeconomic equality (inequality).

Equality as a Cause of Electoral Systems

A parallel line of research, chiefly by economic historians and political scientists, concurs with the association between institutions and equality, but proposes the opposite causal direction: that equality influences institutions. The essence of this argument is that greater income equality broadens political participation and hence contributes to the emergence and survival of democracy. For instance, in his game-theoretic model of political transitions, Boix (2003) attributes both the formation and the duration of democracy to rising income equality. Empirically, Przeworski et al. (2000) find that greater equality (and better economic performance) produces better odds of democratic survival (Przeworski et al. 2000). On the other hand, inequality is found to have the opposite effect: Engerman and Sokoloff (2002) argue that colonial-era income inequality in many Latin American countries has contributed to limited participation and persistent political-economic privileges for the ruling elite down to the present day (Engerman and Sokoloff 2002).

This chapter takes this argument, that rising income equality broadens political participation, one step further: We argue that countries are more likely to adopt (and retain) PR as income equality increases.[6] In the following section,

[6] In the recent literature, Boix (1999) argues that, historically, it was the combination of rising strength of socialists and political fragmentation

Socioeconomic Origins of Electoral Systems

we first develop a simple public finance model of redistribution, based on the setup in Persson and Tabellini (2000), which takes into account voters' income inequality, demand for redistribution, and choice of electoral systems. The key finding is an important (yet commonly neglected) proposition: that aggregated social welfare is maximized by choosing the policy preferred by the *average*, rather than the *median*, voter in the income distribution. Making use of this proposition, we will turn to a spatial model and show that increases in inequality (equality) – because of a growing (reduction in the) gap between the average and the median income voter- will also increase (reduce) the welfare loss in a representative democratic society and hence make majoritarian (PR) systems more desirable.

A Public Finance Model of Redistribution

Replicating much of Persson and Tabellini's setup in their public finance model (2000, chap. 3), which follows in essence the argument originally advanced by Meltzer and Richard (1981), we consider a closed-economy society with the size of population normalized to unity. Citizens in this society,

among conservatives that transformed electoral systems from majoritarianism into PR. Cusack et al. (2007), questioning the validity of Boix's argument, attribute the adoption of PR to the geographical spread of specialized economic interests. In the later section, we will discuss our theory with reference to those related studies.

indexed by i, derive their utility according to the quasi-linear function

$$u^i = \alpha^i c^i + (1 - \alpha^i)H(g) \qquad (1)$$

where c^i is private consumption, g is spending (per capita) on public goods, and $H(.)$ is a continuous and concave function. Note that a citizen's utility is a convex combination of private and public consumption, where the α^i ($\alpha^i \in [0, 1]$) term represents the weight on private consumption. Citizens differ in the relative weight α^i that they put on these two goods, but they do not differ in their valuation of the public good.

Each citizen also differs in the level of income, y^i. Assume y^i follows a cumulative distribution function $F(.)$ with mean y and median y^m. From the empirical regularity that the income distribution is right-skewed, we assume $y^m < y$. The government finances g by imposing a flat-rate tax (t) on each individual's income. Therefore, private consumption differs across individuals

$$c^i = (1 - t)y^i \qquad (2)$$

The government faces a hard budget constraint, and no borrowing or rent-seeking is permitted. In other words, the budget constraint is governed by

$$g = ty \qquad (3)$$

Hence, we can use direct substitution and rewrite the citizen's utility function as

$$u^i = \alpha^i(y - g)(y^i/y) + (1 - \alpha^i)H(g) \qquad (4)$$

It is easy to show that individual i's optimal level of public-goods supply, g^{i*}, is

$$g^{i*} = H_g^{-1}\left[\left(\frac{\alpha^i}{1 - \alpha^i}\right)\left(\frac{y^i}{y}\right)\right] \qquad (5)$$

To demonstrate this result more explicitly (and without the loss of generality), we can use a log function to represent $H(.)$. If we do so, Equation (5) is simplified to

$$g^{i*} = \left(\frac{1 - \alpha^i}{\alpha^i}\right)\left(\frac{y}{y^i}\right) \qquad (6)$$

From Equation (6), we can clearly see that a citizen's preferred level of g decreases in α^i and y^i. Put differently, richer individuals, and those who place more weight on their private consumption, prefer less of the public good and lower taxation. Because we normally assume that richer individuals value public goods less,[7] these two effects should reinforce each other. Note however that the chief result, that demand for public goods decreases with wealth, holds even under the highly adverse assumptions that (a) all citizens weight private

---

[7] A familiar example is public schools: Because the rich can afford private schooling, they value provision of a good public school education less.

and public consumption the same, (b) all government spending is financed by a flat tax, (c) there is no explicit redistribution, only provision of a genuinely public good, and (d) all citizens derive the same utility from the public good. *A fortiori*, it seems self-evident that individual preferences for public spending will decline even more steeply with income when taxes are progressive or redistribution is explicit.

That the rich dislike public spending because of the higher tax burden seems unsurprising. What is crucial to our model is that, by the standard utilitarian criterion, the aggregated social welfare (i.e., the summed welfare of individual citizens) is maximized when (and only when) the welfare of the mean citizen is maximized. To see this mathematically, note that what maximizes the welfare of the mean citizen, $\frac{1}{n}\int_i u^i(r)dF$, obviously maximizes the aggregated social welfare, $\int_i u^i(r)dF$.[8] In other words, the socially optimal level of g^* when $y^i = y$, and under the limiting assumption that $\alpha^i = \alpha$ for all i, is

$$g^* = \left(\frac{1-\alpha}{\alpha}\right)\left(\frac{y}{y}\right) = \frac{1-\alpha}{\alpha} \qquad (7)$$

To elaborate this point, Figure 6.2 plots the aggregated social welfare against the distance between the median income voter (defined as the voter whose preferred point is adopted

---

[8] This point becomes even trivial, given that n has been normalized to unity in our model.

Socioeconomic Origins of Electoral Systems

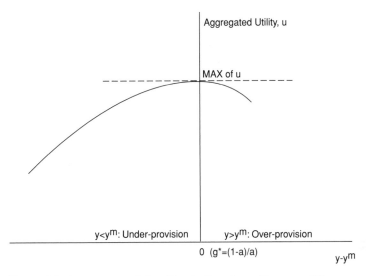

Figure 6.2. Aggregate social welfare as function of income difference between median voter and average citizen.

and represented by the final policy outcome) and the average income citizen. As we can see, given the concavity of the utility function, the aggregated social welfare is maximized when $y^m = y$ (and the corresponding $g^* = \dfrac{1-\alpha}{\alpha}$). As the position of the median voter diverges more from that of the mean citizen, so must the welfare loss from adoption of the preferred policy of the median voter increase.

Recall that the objective of our model is to show that change in inequality can change the welfare consequences of electoral systems. We have just established the first step toward our end: social welfare is maximized when the

preferred policy of the mean citizen is implemented. In practice, however, the actual policy outcome corresponds to the
median voter whose position might or might not coincide
with that of the mean citizen. The welfare loss emerges as
the position of the median voter diverges more from that of
the average citizen.

To move toward the second step of our argument, we need
to know what determines the location of the median voter.
Fortunately, the answer to this question has been persuasively
provided by the work of G. Bingham Powell and others: that
PR systems produce outcomes near the preferred policy of the
median voter, while majoritarian systems lead to the adoption
of policies on average well to the right of the median (Huber
and Powell 1994; Powell 2000, 2002; McDonald et al. 2004). In
the context of our chapter, PR reliably yields the policy (the
one of concern here is the size of redistribution) that is closer
to the ideal point of the median income voter, while majoritarian systems move policy to the right of the median voter and
toward the position of the (richer) mean voter who prefers less
redistribution.[9]

The last (and perhaps obvious) piece of our picture is that
the distance between mean and median increases as income
inequality grows. For the sake of argument, we assume that
the rising income inequality does not change the position of

---

[9] Recall the income distribution is right-skewed, so $y > y^m$.

the median income voter but only moves the mean income in society up to a higher percentile. A familiar example that makes the point vividly is to imagine a society in which all members but one are equally wealthy, and that one – let us call him Bill Gates – is vastly wealthier. The median income, which is not affected by Gates' wealth, will be lower than the mean, which is so affected; and the wealthier Gates becomes, the more the distance between the median income (which will not change) and the mean (which will) increases.

With these points in mind, we argue that when inequality increases – indicated by the growing gap between the mean-income citizen and the median-income voter – the welfare loss will be reduced if the society shifts to a majoritarian system. Similarly, as the mean and the median converge (hence a reduction of income inequality), the initially unequal society might find a shift to PR welfare-improving. Obviously, incentives do not determine results, nor are welfare-improving steps always taken. Following the old political entrepreneur argument of Gary Becker (1983), we simply suggest that, to the extent politicians can appropriate some share of the resultant welfare improvements for themselves, they will be likelier to pursue the institutional change that changing equality stimulates.[10]

---

[10] A commonly accepted, if only parallel, example is that of electoral reform in the nineteenth-century United Kingdom: the Unreformed House of Commons represented a median (landowning) voter who supported

Change and Persistence in Electoral Systems: A Spatial Model

To formalize our argument, we begin our analysis with a (relatively) equal society that uses a PR system. (Because we assume it to be a democracy, all citizens are voters.) We graphically map the policy outcome onto the distribution of income where we identify the relative position of the median and the mean voter. This hypothesized society is represented in Figure 6.3, where we mark the policy desired by the median voter, that desired by the mean voter, that produced by PR systems, and that produced by majoritarian systems, by y^m, y, r^{PR}, and r^{MAJ}, respectively. Note that y^m is located in the middle of the distribution, because it represents the 50th percentile of income; y is located to the right of y^m, because the income distribution is right-skewed. In the initial situation, because the society is relatively equal, the distance between median and mean voter preferences is slight. Also notice that, following our previous discussion, we assume that the mapped policy position under PR systems, r^{PR}, coincides with y^m, and that the mapped policy position under majoritarian systems, r^{MAJ}, is located to the right of r^{PR}.

grain tariffs and opposed taxpayer-funded municipal improvements. As the average (mercantile or manufacturing) citizen increasingly diverged from the limited-franchise median, and inflicted growing welfare costs, incentives grew for political leaders to broaden the franchise and bring the median voter closer to the average citizen. The result was a succession of Reform Acts, beginning in 1832.

Socioeconomic Origins of Electoral Systems

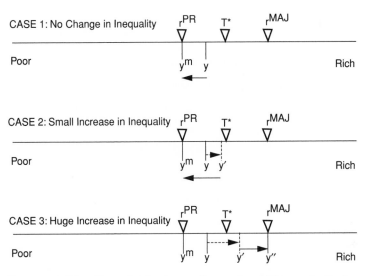

Figure 6.3. The effect of rising inequality on the shift to majoritarian systems in an equal society.

Let us assume that this society remains static and is immune from any external shock. In this case (Case 1 in Figure 6.3) we expect two consequences. First, compared to r^{MAJ}, r^{PR} is closer to y, so the society will endure less welfare loss if it sticks with PR (recall that the welfare loss increases as the policy position diverges more from that of the mean voter). Therefore, the society has no incentive to deviate and PR is sustained. Secondly, due to the redistributive nature of PR, PR contributes to a more equal society and the gap between y and y^m is reduced (as indicated by the direction of the dashed arrow). The increase of income equality and the resultant convergence between r^{PR} and y make the continuation of PR even more appealing, which in turn strengthens the existing preference for PR.

Now, imagine that this society is exposed to some exogenous shock, and that income inequality increases as a result.[11] What would happen to the society's preferences among electoral systems, then? The answer depends on the magnitude of the shock and accordingly, how far y is pushed away from y^m. Let T^* (the "threshold") denote the midpoint between r^{PR} and r^{MAJ}, and the upshot is that as long as y stays within $[r^{PR}, T^*]$, PR will remain welfare-superior. However, if the external shock is huge enough to push y to the right of T^*, then the society as a whole (or, equivalently, a benevolent social planner), reevaluating the welfare consequences under alternative electoral systems, will rationally prefer a majoritarian system.

To see this point, suppose a minor external shock occurs and moves the position of the mean income voter slightly upward. This new scenario is represented in Case 2 in Figure 6.3, where the dashed arrow moves the mean voter's income position from y to y'. Under such circumstances, due to the upward shift of y, the policy produced by the existing PR system incurs higher welfare loss than before. However, PR is still welfare-superior and is maintained by the society.

[11] A classic example would be the opening of a labor-scarce economy to greater international trade: for a convincing real-world example, see O'Rourke and Williamson (1999, chap. 4).

This is because the distance between y' and r^{PR} is still shorter than that between y' and r^{MAJ}. In other words, if one shifted to a majoritarian system, the welfare loss resulting from the new redistribution policy, r^{MAJ}, would be even higher than the current welfare loss caused by r^{PR}. So PR is rationally maintained as the lesser evil. Moreover, if the society stops experiencing further increase in income inequality, then again, the redistributive nature of PR will gradually drag y' back toward y^m (as shown by the direction of the solid arrow) and offset the income inequality caused by the external shock. The long-term equilibrium will be near Case 1, where PR equalizes the society and the social preference for PR reinforces PR's persistence.

Finally, suppose the society experiences a huge increase in inequality (as shown by the direction of the dashed arrow in Case 3), moving the position of the average income voter, y, to y''. In this case, the distance between y'' and r^{PR} is longer than that between y' and r^{MAJ}, so the initial welfare loss caused by r^{PR} is higher than the one that would be caused by r^{MAJ}. Therefore, the society has an incentive to shift from PR to the majoritarian system because the electoral reform reduces the welfare loss. Importantly, if the society once chooses a majoritarian system, the fact that majoritarian systems tend to redistribute less will further increase income inequality, pushing y'' away from y (and even closer to r^{MAJ} as shown by the direction of the solid arrow).

The dynamic processes suggested in Figure 6.3 underscore the argument in this study: An equal society prefers PR to majoritarian systems because of the welfare advantage, and PR is self-sustaining and resistant to a small increase in inequality. However, when experiencing a great increase in inequality, the society has incentives to abandon its old PR system and adopt a majoritarian one because the new policy produced by majoritarian systems will make the society better off from a social welfare perspective.

The same logic of social welfare maximization applies to the opposite situation. At the risk of repetition, we depict the causal dynamic for a highly unequal society in Figure 6.4. As we can clearly see, the unequal society has a strong interest in installing and maintaining majoritarian systems, and the majoritarian system in turn increases inequality. In addition, when there is no change or only a small decrease in inequality, the majoritarian system is maintained (Case 4 and Case 5). Lastly, the society finds it welfare-improving to change to PR only when it experiences a large decrease in inequality (Case 6).

Again, we emphasize that welfare-improvement is not the whole story, and that – as political obstacles to free trade repeatedly demonstrate – obviously welfare-improving reforms are often blocked by organized interests. Among many other factors that might matter for outcomes, where producers, who benefit from PR, are well-organized in trade

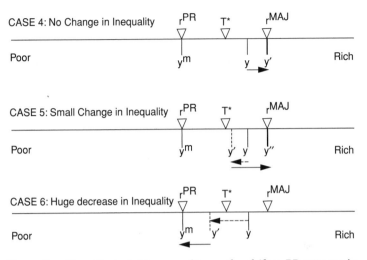

Figure 6.4. The effect of rising equality on the shift to PR systems in an unequal society

unions and industry associations – and this is particularly likely to be the case, as Wallerstein (1989) showed, in smaller countries – the switch to PR will be easier and its abandonment harder.

Empirical Testing

We extend the data provided by Boix (1999) to test our hypotheses. To the best of our knowledge, Boix's is the first systematic study that uses quantitative data to investigate the origin of electoral systems crossnationally.[12] In his

---

[12] Note that, in her pioneering study, Bawn (1993) analyzes the logic underlying the choice of electoral rule in Germany.

elegant study, Boix seeks to understand what factors affect the choice of electoral rules for opportunistic incumbents. To answer this question, he assembles a sample of twenty-two democratic countries during the interwar years,[13] and he captures the distinction between PR and majoritarian systems by using the "effective electoral threshold" (EET) as the dependent variable. Technically, the EET measures " ... the proportion of votes that, for each electoral system, secures parliamentary representation to any party with a probability of at least 50 percent" (Boix 1999, 614). Intuitively, it measures how difficult it is for a party to obtain seats in parliament and hence taps into the degree of majoritarianism. The value of EET is lower under PR and is higher under majoritarian systems. We follow Boix and use EET as the dependent variable.[14]

We begin our empirical analysis by first trying to replicate Boix's study. As the results in Model 1 of Table 6.1 show clearly,

---

[13] They are: Australia (1919–39), Austria (1919–34), Belgium (1919–34), Canada (1919–39), Denmark (1919–39), Finland (1919–39), France (1919–39), Germany (1919–33), Greece (1923–36), Iceland (1934–39), Ireland (1922–39), Italy (1919–23), Japan (1925–40), Luxembourg (1919–39), the Netherlands (1919–39), New Zealand (1919–39), Norway (1919–39), Spain (1931–36), Sweden (1919–39), Switzerland (1919–39), the UK (1919–39), and the United States (1919–39). Later in his study, he supplements his sample with nine extra countries from after 1945, and his substantive results remain unchanged.

[14] For detailed description and the temporal variation of EET, see Boix (1999, 614–16).

212

Socioeconomic Origins of Electoral Systems

Table 6.1. Estimation results

The dependent variable	Model 1 EET	Model 2 EET	Model 3 EET FARM1938
THREAT	−.131***		−.096*
	[.030]		[.049]
ΔFARM		−.860**	−.887**
		[.303]	[.329]
FARM1918			.838***
			[.074]
EET			−.366**
			[.157]
lnPOP			−2.144*
			[1.078]
Fragmentation ×	−33.647***		−19.075
Area Dummy	[10.898]		[13.797]
Constant	28.511***	27.712***	36.616***
	[3.735]	[5.140]	[4.809]
N; R2	22; .401	18; .239	18; .439

Note: Because of the omission of main effects, Models 1 and 3 are misspecified and likely biased. As our purpose is to replicate Table 3 in Boix (1999) as closely as possible, we nevertheless use his specification.

this chapter corroborates his main findings.[15] The key independent variable in Boix's study, THREAT, represents the joint effect of the strength of rising socialism and the coordination capability among the conservative ruling elites. Boix argues that the coefficient of THREAT should be negative, because

---

[15] We use the data provided in the appendix to Boix's article. While the numerical results do not appear exactly the same because THREAT is scaled differently, the results are substantively identical.

countries with strong socialist parties and fragmented conservative forces are more likely to adopt PR. Our results accord with Boix's.

To test the effect of increases in inequality on electoral systems, we first need a proxy for income inequality. The most common indexes for income inequality, such as the Gini index reported by Deininger and Squire, are unfortunately not widely available for the interwar period covered by Boix's data set. In his subsequent study, Boix (2003) therefore adopts two of Vanhanen's indices (1997) to capture income inequality before World War II: the distribution of agricultural property and the quality of human capital.

Vanhanen (1997) measures the distribution of agricultural property by calculating the share of total agricultural holdings held by family farms. As measured by decade beginning with 1858, Vanhanen defines family farms as ones that have less than four employees (including family members) and that are primarily cultivated by the family itself. As Boix (2003) notes, this definition differentiates family farms from large and professional farms that are cultivated by hired workers, and hence provides a good proxy for the degree of land concentration. In other words, countries with a higher percentage of family farms enjoy a higher degree of equality in land ownership. Given the centrality of land ownership and agricultural property to a family's income in the prewar period, we believe that measuring inequality through the percentage of family farms is justified on strong theoretical grounds. Empirically, the percentage of family farms also seems to tap into income inequality very well. Boix reports that for the postwar period for which both the Gini index and Vanhanen's family farm indicator are available, the correlation between these two indexes is moderately high (−.66) (Boix 2003, 90).

The second proxy for income inequality that Boix suggests is Vanhanen's index of knowledge distribution. Put loosely, this index is based on the mean share of literates and students in the adult population. However, we believe that, unlike the distribution of agricultural property, the theoretical linkage between knowledge distribution and income inequality is less clear during the prewar period. Moreover, preliminary analysis suggests that the variable of knowledge distribution does not significantly affect the electoral system, especially once the agricultural property variable is taken into consideration. Hence, we drop the variable of knowledge distribution and proceed with only the variable of family farms variable as our indicator of income inequality.

Consistent with the time period examined in this chapter, we take the values of the family farms variable in both the 1930s (with the 1938 term) and 1910s (with the 1918 term), and we let the difference represent the change in inequality from the 1910s to 1930s. The resultant variable, ΔFARM, ranges from 1 to 26 and has a mean of 10.9 and a standard deviation of 7.8. This indicates that from the 1910s to 1930s, there was a general trend toward increasing equality of agricultural holdings.[16] Note that Austria, Iceland, Ireland, and Luxembourg do not have information on this variable, reducing our sample size to eighteen. Therefore, the issue of degrees of freedom forces us to rely on a stylized empirical model rather than a fully specified one.

To test our hypothesis that an increase in equality (inequality) makes it more likely that a society will adopt a PR (majoritarian) system, Model 2 replaces Boix's threat variable with ΔFARM, and the estimated coefficient of ΔFARM turns out to be negative, as expected, and highly significant ($t = -2.8$). This result also vouches for an almost one-to-one effect of change in inequality on electoral systems: as the proportion of family farms increases by 1 percent (i.e., greater equality), the proportion of votes that a party needs to secure parliamentary seats is reduced by 0.86 percent (i.e., becomes less majoritarian). On the other side of the token, one can easily infer that an increase in inequality results in a system that is more majoritarian.

That an increase in equality (inequality) leads to more proportional (majoritarian) systems is only half of the picture. To test our main hypothesis that electoral systems are self-sustaining, we construct a nonrecursive model that

---

[16] This accords with many other measures of increasing equality, albeit on a smaller set of countries, in the interwar period: see particularly Atkinson and Piketty (2007).

contains two equations.[17] The first equation combines Model 1 and Model 2, and relates the electoral system variable to the variables of threat and change in income inequality. The second equation conversely tests whether income inequality in the 1930s (proxied as FARM1938) is dependent on electoral system (EET), after controlling for the initial inequality condition in the 1910s (FARM1918).[18] It also controls for a country's population size because to a certain extent it is harder to maintain socioeconomic equity in populous states.

The results in Model 3 strongly support our hypothesis. First, we can see that the electoral system exerts a strong redistributive effect: As the electoral threshold increases, income equality, represented by the proportion of family farms, deteriorates. Put differently, our empirical results corroborate the conventional wisdom that PR (majoritarian) systems are associated with greater (less) redistribution. Second, an increase in equality (inequality) continues to strengthen social preference for PR (majoritarian) systems. Perhaps even more importantly, Model 3 shows that on top of the political mechanism identified by Boix, the socioeconomic forces play at least

---

[17] The model is estimated via full three-stage least squares, and a small-sample adjustment is made.

[18] The reason for controlling for the initial condition is obvious: there is more room for an equal society to become polarized than an already unequal society.

an equally important role in shaping the formation and persistence of electoral systems. This suggests, at least to us, an account of electoral-system change that (a) is more strategic and less tactical than that of Boix (1999) and (b) favors the more parsimonious account of Boix (2003) over the more complicated one of Boix (1999).

Discussion

The previous empirical analysis, derived from our theoretical model, underscores the main points of our study: Electoral systems, as we observe, are normally self-sustaining and change little over time. Importantly, big changes of electoral systems are driven by exogenous shocks (such as wars, globalizations, and demographic or technological revolutions) that affect socioeconomic inequality. Particularly, an increase in equality increases the likelihood that PR will be adopted, while rising inequality favors a switch to (or retention of) majoritarian systems.

Our finding links this chapter directly to some recent studies that investigate the institutional consequence of income inequality. Rogowski and MacRae (2008) examine how shifts in social and economic inequality resulting from changes in economic and military technology, trade, and factor endowments shape politicians' incentives to broaden or restrict political participation. However, unlike Rogowski and MacRae

(2008), which focuses the effect of income inequality on political enfranchisement, this study deals with both persistence of and change in electoral systems. The finding of this chapter is congruent with Ticchi and Vindigni (2010), who argue that increasing equality in many countries during the twentieth century was associated with the shift to PR; while increasing inequality in recent years may push for a change to majoritarian methods of election. However, we propose an alternative and, in our view a more plausible, mechanism. In Ticchi and Vindigni's model, the median voter chooses the electoral system. Citizens are divided into three classes; the rich always favor majoritarian systems and the middle class always choose PR on the (to us unlikely) assumption that under majoritarian rule the poor will always vote for a rich candidate. The group that delivers the final verdict on electoral systems is the poor, who prefer PR only when the income distribution is highly unequal. In our study, the mechanism that does the work is the redistributive consequences of electoral systems and politicians' indirect incentives to maximization social welfare.

This chapter also relates to an emerging literature that seeks to understand the origin of electoral systems. As discussed earlier, Boix argues that existing right-wing parties chose PR when they were politically fragmented and were strongly challenged by the rising socialist movement. The reason is that, when existing right-wing parties are fragmented, their supporters will find it hard to coordinate and remain united. With a strong socialist challenge, the fragmented right-wing parties are very likely to suffer a huge electoral loss if they do not shift to PR, where their existing supporter basis can be preserved.

Boix's logic, however, appears problematic. As Cusack et al. note, Boix does not entertain the possibility of electoral alliances among the conservatives. Importantly, once they enrich Boix's model to a more realistic game where they consider redistributive spending across different groups under different electoral systems, they argue that it is implausible that the right wing would ever choose PR. Their criticisms appear largely valid; and, as our empirical results in Model 3 indicate, once we factor in the redistributive consequence of electoral systems, the variable of THREAT becomes insignificant. Hence, rather than the combined effect of fragmented conservativism and rising socialism, Cusack et al. argue that the key to understanding the historical transition to PR lies in the expansion of specialized economic interests induced by the process of industrialization and urbanization. Their industrialization argument, while distinct from ours, falls squarely with our emphasis on change caused by external shocks.

Other recent contributions along the line of endogenizing electoral systems include Andrews and Jackman (2005),

Benoit (2004), and Blais et al. (2004)[19] where several plausible determinants, such as uncertainty, anticipated electoral gains, and the spread of democratic ideas, have been explicitly addressed. While informative, their emphasis is largely on exploring what factors contribute to the transition from majoritarian systems to PR, and hence their scope is somewhat limited. This chapter moves the literature a step farther by providing a socioeconomic account that can also explain the transition from PR to majoritarian systems (we speculate, for example, that the recent adoption of SMD in Italy and Japan may reflect rises in inequality). The theory of self-reinforcing electoral systems proposed in this chapter also enhances our understanding on the persistence of electoral systems.

Conclusion

Because of their far-reaching political and economic consequences, issues of electoral systems have spawned much exciting research over the past few years. Crudely summarized, studies of electoral systems have been developed in two parallel fashions. On the one hand, electoral systems are taken as given, and different electoral systems are found to affect

---

[19] The list of literature is not intended to be exhaustive.

voter turnout, cabinet stability, government duration, partisanship of the government, composition of governmental expenditures, budgetary deficits, prices, and income inequality. On the other hand, growing scholarly attention has been devoted to the endogeneity of electoral systems, with a special emphasis on the choice of electoral systems and the causes of electoral reform. This chapter seeks to integrate these two seemingly unconnected lines of scholarship into a unifying framework. We posit that a self-reinforcing cycle connects electoral systems and socioeconomic inequality. Specifically, in agreement with the existing theoretical and empirical literature, we argue that countries with PR systems are associated with left-wing (Center–Left) governments and extensive redistribution. Meanwhile, we posit that PR systems, due to their lower seats-votes elasticity, are found to restrain economic competition and increase the real price in favor of producers. These forces jointly lead to greater equality of incomes in a society. This high income equality, sustained by higher wages and generous labor policies, in turn either gives rise to PR or reinforces societal preferences for existing PR systems. We present evidence supporting our claim. The self-reinforcing cycle proposed in this study provides a plausible account for institutional stability, and significantly enriches our understanding of electoral systems' short-term effects and their long-term evolutionary dynamics.

7

Conclusion

The fundamental claim of this book has been just this: that more responsive political systems – ones that shift the most power in response to the smallest changes in voter sentiment – empower consumers. The less the distribution of power responds to voter sentiment, the more powerful producers will be. And because producers readily conspire to inhibit competition, that power expresses itself in anticompetitive policies: barriers to entry, regulated prices, local or niche-market monopolies. Although we have focused on one (we believe) particularly compelling bit of evidence, namely the link between electoral systems and prices, our more basic point has many further implications, some of which we outline here as an agenda for further research.

If our basic point is right, electoral systems must be endogenous (as Acemoglu [2005] has argued, and as we have tried to show in Chapter 6): Neither voters nor politicians (let alone lobbyists) are fools, and they understand (if only intuitively) a great deal of what is at stake. Yet crucial political institutions are "sticky," indeed often constitutionally anchored, and we will follow convention in positing in the first part of our discussion here that the electoral system is exogenous. So what, beyond higher prices, does a *less* responsive electoral system (in most cases, PR) entail? At a minimum, we argue, quite different modes of political action and organization, different fiscal systems, and consequently different policies.

If Institutions Are Exogenous

Political Organization

(1) Because votes make little difference, lobbyists in PR systems will not seek to influence voters directly: they will waste few resources on the kinds of **political action committees** that try to sway Americans' or Britons' votes.[1] Rather, lobbyists will contribute directly to parties or politicians, or will seek elite influence predominantly by other channels (charities, lavish entertainment, spectacular events, nepotism).

(2) Just as "the tariff was mother of the trust" (as nineteenth- and early twentieth-century radicals put it), so the availability of pro-producer policies under low-responsiveness government stimulates and preserves **powerful producer organizations**: at the sectoral level, the national

---

[1] We owe this insight to David Laitin.

Conclusion

level, or even (e.g., within the European Union) supranational level – or sometimes all three at once. Low-responsiveness politics engenders strong organizations of both owners and workers and encourages labor-management cooperation ("corporatism") that both ensures monopoly profits and guarantees a "fair" division of those profits. So strong do these organizations sometimes become that major political parties are often mere coalitions of interest groups (e.g., Germany's Christian Democratic Union in its formative years: see Domes [1964]).

Higher Wages, Greater Equality, Better Training

(3) In democracies, low-responsiveness politics and resultant anticompetitive policies serve (somewhat paradoxically) to **strengthen labor, raise organized-sector wages, and reduce economic inequality** – although the reduction in inequality holds only among "insiders" (more on this later) and fades in the face of immigration or global cheap-labor competition.

PR's disempowerment of voters and encouragement of strong organizations helps all producers (certainly including managers) but actually helps labor more. Once both management and labor are strongly organized, unions easily become the dominant "social partners," capable both of disrupting the economy and (at least where centralized) of commanding a bloc of votes big enough to affect outcomes even

225

in low-responsiveness systems. The powerful unions then win higher wages[2] (especially for the more numerous low-skill workers), either at the direct expense of consumers (in trade-sheltered sectors) or indirectly via higher social benefits (in sectors where international competition inhibits pass-through of higher costs to consumers). The end result, at least where much of labor is organized, is (as argued earlier) **greater economic equality**.

(4) Once achieved, monopoly profits and high wages can be sustained (i.e., not competed away) only by erecting elaborate **barriers to entry**: daunting technical qualifications, long apprenticeships, restrictive licensure.[3] On this, workers and owners find common ground: difficult qualifications and licensure both restrict the supply of new workers and (if training is good) assure employers that new workers' marginal product will more closely approximate their high wage. Thus it is not so surprising (e.g., in Germany) that unions and employers have repeatedly been able to renegotiate and preserve the elaborate training systems that guarantee a highly qualified (and quite expensive) workforce (Thelen 2004, chaps. 2 and 5).

---

[2] More precisely: wages that exceed the relevant workers' marginal product, i.e., that must somehow be subsidized.

[3] We do not at all exclude the possibility that the preexistence of strong producer organizations (e.g., guilds) predisposes a country toward PR (cf. Cusack, Iversen, and Soskice 2007). We take up this theme in earnest when, later, we begin to treat the electoral system as endogenous.

Conclusion

(5) More darkly, the barriers to entry usually guarantee **insider-outsider** distinctions (Rueda 2005, 2007) and significant **gender and ethnic discrimination**. The benefits to labor under the pro-producer regime go only to *organized* workers, creating a classical "dual labor market" and actually pushing down wages in any unorganized branches. As some close students of "organized market economies" have noted, too often unions and employers can agree that the high training costs of a long and demanding apprenticeship would be "wasted" on women (too likely to interrupt their careers for family reasons); hence the high-skill, well-paid workforce tends to be overwhelmingly male, while women are consigned (even in professedly egalitarian societies) to the low-wage, unorganized sectors (Estevez-Abe, Iversen, and Soskice 2001). A similar logic can be used against "less reliable" minorities, or ones who may objectively be more likely to return, temporarily or permanently, to their homelands, and thus to "export" any investment in their human capital.

Consumption Taxes, Inefficient Retailing

The disempowerment of consumers in low-responsiveness systems is expressed baldly in two kinds of policies: A strong bias toward **taxes on consumption** rather than on labor (income) or capital (property, capital gains, corporations); and toleration, indeed legal protection, of **extremely**

inefficient retailing (small shops, local monopolies, restricted opening hours, retail price maintenance, etc.).

(6) Owners reject taxes on capital and corporate income; managers oppose highly progressive income taxes; workers dislike taxes on labor. All producer groups can agree on **taxing consumers**, provided only (a) that the sums raised finance social benefits (which flow mostly to workers) and (b) that sales abroad (exports) are not taxed.[4] While it is also the case that well-structured consumption taxes (e.g., a value-added tax) are less distortionary, particularly in highly trade-exposed economies, even controlling for these effects we expect less responsive political systems to derive a higher proportion of government revenues from taxes on consumption.[5] Or, to put it the other way around: to the extent that a responsive political system empowers consumers, they will have the "clout" to minimize taxes on consumption.

---

[4] The pioneering and absolutely indispensable article on this point (which happens also to be consistent with our argument here) is Baramendi and Rueda 2007.

[5] Of twelve OECD countries on which effective tax rates on consumption are available for 1995, six happened to use PR and six majoritarian electoral systems. Among the PR systems, effective tax rates on consumption ranged from 16.7 to 32.9 percent, with an average of 24.6 percent; the majoritarian systems ranged from 5.6 to 19.9 percent, with an average of 13.2 percent (Baramendi and Rueda 2007, 622, table 1). The alert reader may now wonder whether consumption taxes do not account for all of the price differences that we observe between PR and majoritarian systems. They do not. We have rigorously checked for this possibility at earlier stages of our research, e.g., in Chapter 3.

Conclusion

(7) Offered the identical product at radically different prices by two otherwise equal retailers, the rational consumer will always choose the lower price: indeed, in strict competition theory the higher-price retailer will wind up with zero sales. Hence, competitive retailing leads repeatedly to radical improvements in efficiency that permit innovative retailers to offer the same goods at lower prices: The mom-and-pop store yields to the supermarket, the supermarket to Wal-Mart; and each wave has granted consumers the same (or better) goods at ever-lower real prices.[6] Governmental policy however can spur, retard, or prohibit competition in a hugely inventive variety of ways, from strict regulation of interstate trucking or banking (the United States for many years) or airlines (most countries until the 1970s), to grants of local monopolies to bakeries and pharmacies (Germany until quite recently), to restrictions on the physical size of shops (France), the number of outlets that any one firm or individual can own (German pharmacies), the hours during which stores may be open for business, the prices they may charge (German bookstores), or the wages their sector must pay ("privatized" German postal delivery). More recently, barriers have gone up

---

[6] Typically, the arrival of a Wal-Mart store in a community "reduces consumer prices for food by fully 25 percent, of which 20 percent is the direct Wal-Mart impact and the other 5 percent represents the response of local stores to the Wal-Mart arrival." Hausman and Leibtag 2004, as cited in Gorden and Dew-Becker 2008.

against Web-based retailing, particularly from extraterritorial sources (Canadian online pharmacies in the United States, Dutch ones in Germany).

Retailers, like most humans, prefer a predictable and comfortable existence, hence (see again Adam Smith) are always eager to ban precisely the kind of "cutthroat competition" that spurs innovation and lowers retail prices. Producers are at best indifferent, or – where, as with Wal-Mart, aggressive retailers use their market power to demand wholesale price cuts – actively sympathize with the more traditional retailers. Only consumers fully benefit from retail innovation. Thus, where low-responsiveness political systems restrict consumers' influence, policy remains strongly anticompetitive, retailing retains ancient inefficiencies, and retail prices (depending on the extent of the restriction) range from high to extortionate.[7]

Concretely, then: We expect that, under low-responsiveness electoral systems, retailing will remain a particularly inefficient, highly regulated, and high-cost sector. Any shift from PR to a majoritarian system will tend to produce more competitive and efficient retailing; any shift from a

---

[7] Many non-Europeans have experienced the literal headache of discovering that the same over-the-counter painkillers that retail for about 2 U.S. cents per tablet in much of the world cost about twenty times that much in highly regulated European pharmacies.

Conclusion

majoritarian system to PR will quickly induce more regulation, less competition, and greater inefficiency.

Longer Time-Horizons, Better Infrastructure

(8) On the brighter side, and as others have noted, low-responsiveness systems, precisely by shielding politicians from shifting currents of popular opinion, allow leaders **longer time-horizons** and **greater intertemporal credibility**. Thus PR systems, if securely in place, create a more favorable environment for long-term infrastructural investment. Just as James Rauch (Rauch 1995) has found among U.S. cities, governmental systems that assure leaders longer and more secure tenure (in that case, professional city-manager systems) lead to markedly greater investment in appropriate infrastructure (streets, sewers, harbors, airports) and hence, all else equal, to greater investment and growth; so low-responsiveness systems, for all their disadvantages in competitiveness and prices, should lead (or so we hypothesize for future research) to more and better infrastructure, and (perhaps) to the kind of policy commitment that reassures investors.[8]

---

[8] All else equal, the better infrastructure should lower costs, but in an anticompetitive environment this simply increases oligopoly slack rather than lowering prices.

Electoral Systems and Balance of Consumer-Producer Power

Summarizing our discussion so far: If we could take political institutions, and in particular the electoral system, as exogenous, our model would lead to the further implication that low-responsiveness systems would inspire:

- a higher degree of political organization,
- a style of lobbying centered on parties and leaders rather than on voters,
- higher wages, far more emphasis on workforce training and qualification, and (until low-wage international competition becomes significant) greater equality;
- at the same time, greater discrimination against women and minorities;
- greater reliance on consumption taxes
- greater regulation of, and inefficiency in, retailing; but also
- greater investment in infrastructure.

All of this (and more) would follow if institutions were completely exogenous, and in the short term, they may ordinarily be taken as such. Institutions can, however, be changed – in some cases by simple law, in others by super-majority or constitutional amendment, in extreme cases by coup or revolution – and sometimes are (in some countries more readily than others[9]). Even in the most conservative

---

[9] Fourth Republic France, even in its short existence, became notorious for frequent, and tactically motivated, changes in its electoral system. The

democracies, however, dysfunctional institutions generate strong incentives for their own change, rewarding the political entrepreneurs whose reforms can reduce inertial and dead-weight costs. And, of course, interests within each system seek institutional changes that will benefit them. If, in this light, we admit that over the longer run institutions are shaped by social forces – but bearing in mind the shorter-term effects we have outlined previously – we must now consider variables that will affect the institutions a country adopts and retains.

Admitting that Institutions Are Endogenous

Preexisting Strength of Producer Organizations; Major War, Country Size

(1) Where producers were, for whatever reason, already highly organized at the inception of democratic institutions, or where some external shock greatly strengthened them, low-responsiveness, pro-producer institutions – particularly the combination of PR and parliamentarism – were much likelier to be adopted and retained. Thus, as many previous students have noted, PR came more easily to countries with a history of **strong guilds**, strong trade unions, powerful employer associations, or (most favorably of all) centralized wage bargaining

recent vacillations in the Italian electoral system have been outlined in Chapter 5.

that brought most of these players regularly to a common table (see, among many others, Katzenstein 1985; Verdier 2001, 2002; Hall and Soskice 2001; Cusack, Iversen, and Soskice 2007). And, of course, the countries that further strengthened these economic institutions under PR-parliamentary government were all the likelier to retain precisely that system.

(2) From this standpoint, the timing of PR's widespread adoption in the years during or immediately after **major wars** (in particular, World War I) makes eminent sense. Major war – certainly among the belligerents, and to some extent even by its effects on neighboring countries – itself creates much stronger producer organizations to manage and discipline the wartime economy: Unions, industry-wide associations, transportation networks – all are integrated into the war effort but at the same time greatly strengthened (even in so unlikely a case as Imperial Germany in World War I; Feldman 1966).

(3) This perspective, we submit, just as simply explains the frequently observed fact that **small countries** more readily adopt and retain PR (Katzenstein 1985). Given the diseconomies of scale in organization (Wallerstein 1989), smaller countries will be more highly organized – not only in trade unions, but in virtually all sectors; and these strong producer organizations will back low-responsiveness, pro-producer institutions. This should be true even when one controls (as we have done in our empirical work) for the extent of

countries' dependence on foreign trade – which tends, of course, to be greater in smaller countries (see further discussion of the trade issue later).

This insight has an important dynamic implication, particularly relevant given recent history: When a smaller country is carved out of a larger one (e.g., by breakup or secession), the new smaller entity is more likely (albeit perhaps with some lag) to adopt PR.

Preexisting Equality

(4) As argued in Chapter 6, PR-parliamentary institutions are likelier to be adopted and retained in societies that – controlling for such aspects as guild history and country size, just mentioned – already exhibit a **high degree of equality** in income and ownership. At least two further reasons are involved: (a) As noted earlier in this chapter, low-responsiveness institutions, by encouraging or reinforcing organizations of workers, tend themselves to have a strong equalizing effect, one that looms as too big a threat to elites in highly unequal societies (cf. Boix 2003). (b) As argued elsewhere (Rogowski and Macrae 2008), as society grows more unequal, PR represents less well the interests of the mean voter, thus likely further reducing social welfare. To put the same point the other way around, the welfare loss from PR is less the more equal the society.

Openness to Trade

(5) The more easily any good or service is traded cross-nationally, the more will the "Law of One Price" obtain: Gold, to take the classical example, commands almost exactly the same real price in every national market, while bricks or haircuts – both extreme examples of nontraded goods – can vary substantially in real price in different countries, and indeed in different locales within countries. And countries themselves differ in their openness to foreign trade, for reasons both of policy (some are more protectionist) and of natural endowment (some have porous borders or natural harbors, others are landlocked or rimmed by almost unsurpassable mountains). Thus, all else equal, anticompetitive arrangements and high real prices will prove harder to defend in those countries (and, as well, in those sectors within countries) characterized by the **greatest share of foreign trade in production and consumption**. And this is exactly what our empirical work has shown: controlling both for country size (which of course is inversely related to trade openness, i.e., small countries tend to trade more) and for political institutions, we find consistently that greater openness to foreign trade is associated with lower real prices, that is, the international market forces "world" prices onto countries and sectors that are more open.

For us, this raises the interesting point of a possible link between "globalization," or increasing openness of

Conclusion

economies, and both anticompetitive policies and nonresponsive institutions. While it is historically true that many countries (particularly small ones) with a high degree of exposure to foreign trade have adopted and retained low-responsiveness institutions, our own conjecture – although, at this point, it is only that – is that such institutions will come under increasing pressure as exposure to international competition affects more and more of their sectors. To reduce this conjecture, finally, almost to a slogan: *globalization ultimately undermines PR* (and similarly less responsive institutions).

Summing up, again: When we view institutions as endogenous, we find that one "inherited" factor and four "changeable" ones affect the likelihood that low-responsiveness institutions will be adopted or retained. The major "inherited" factor favoring PR is:

- a history of strong guilds.

Another, frequently taken as inherited but proven by recent history to be changeable, is:

- small country size.

Two clearly changeable factors favoring PR, which taken together can explain many of the electoral system changes over the last century and more, are:

- major wars and
- greater equality.

The last changeable factor, which ultimately (we conjecture) undermines PR, is:

- **openness to international trade**, or (in its dynamic sense) "globalization."

Since at least the 1860s, students of politics have investigated and debated the effects of electoral systems. More recently, the spotlight has turned to these systems' impacts on governments' economic policies, including particularly their propensity to expand public spending and to inflate the currency. Much more recently, indeed only over the past decade or so, scholars have turned their attention to the possible causes of electoral systems, and in a few cases[10] have begun to think through the possibly reciprocal relationship between electoral and economic system. Part of that overall consideration, in our view, must be the reciprocal link between political institutions and (a) the producer-consumer balance, or (b) the extent to which policy favors, or inhibits, competition. This book, we hope, has advanced precisely that aspect of the overall discussion.

---

[10] The most important contributor here has been Torben Iversen, together with various coauthors.

Bibliography

Acemoglu, Daron. 2005. "Constitutions, Politics, and Economics: A Review Essay on Persson and Tabellini's *The Economic Effects of Constitutions.*" *Journal of Economic Literature* 43: 1025–48.

Adserà, Alícia, Carles Boix, and Mark Payne. 2003. "Are You Being Served? Political Accountability and Quality of Government." *Journal of Law, Economics, & Organization* 19(2): 445–90.

Agresti, Alan. 2002. *Categorical Data Analysis*. Hoboken, NJ: John Wiley & Sons.

Alesina, Alberto, Edward Glaeser and Bruce Sacerdote. 2001. "Why Doesn't the United States Have a European-Style Welfare State?" *Brookings Papers on Economics Activity*, 187–278. Fall.

Alvey, James E. 2000. "The 1999 Election in New Zealand." *IPA Review* 52(1): 17–18. http://www.ipa.org.au/library/review52-1%20The%201999%20Election%20in%20NZ.pdf

Anderson, Christopher J., and Yuliya V. Tverdova. 2003. "Corruption, Political Allegiances, and Attitudes toward Government in Contemporary Democracies." *American Journal of Political Science* 47(1): 91–109.

Andrews, Josephine T., and Robert W. Jackman. 2005. "Strategic Fools: Electoral Rule Choice under Extreme Uncertainty." *Electoral Studies* 24(1): 65–84.

Ansolabehere, Stephen, David Brady, and Morris Fiorina. 1992. "The Vanishing Marginals and Electoral Responsiveness." *British Journal of Political Science* 22(1): 21–38.

Arellano, Manuel, and Stephen Bond. 1991. "Some Tests of Specification for Panel Data: Monte Carlo Evidence and an Application to Employment Equations." *Review of Economic Studies* 58(2): 277–97.

Bibliography

Atkinson, Anthony B., and Thomas Piketty, eds. 2007. *Top Incomes over the Twentieth Century: A Contrast Between Continental European and English-Speaking Countries.* Oxford: Oxford University Press.

Austen-Smith, David. 2000. "Redistributing Income under Proportional Representation." *Journal of Political Economy* 108(6): 1235–69.

Bagehot, Walter. 2004[1867]. *The English Constitution.* Kila, MT: Kessinger Publishing.

Baltagi, Badi. 2001. *Econometric Analysis of Panel Data,* 2nd edition. New York: John Wiley & Sons.

Barro, Robert J. 1999. "Determinants of Democracy." *Journal of Political Economy* 107(6): S158–83.

Barro, Robert J., and Xavier Sala-i-Martin. 1995. *Economic Growth.* New York: McGraw Hill.

Bartels, Larry M., and John Zaller. 2001. "Presidential Vote Models: A Recount." *PS: Political Science & Politics* 34(1): 9–20.

Bates, Robert H. 1981. *Markets and States in Tropical Africa: The Political Basis of Agricultural Policies.* Berkeley, CA: University of California Press.

Bates, Robert H. 1997. *Open-Economy Politics: The Political Economy of the World Coffee Trade.* Princeton, NJ: Princeton University Press.

Bawn, Kathleen. 1993. "The Logic of Institutional Preferences: German Electoral Law as a Social Choice Outcome." *American Journal of Political Science* 37(4): 965–89.

Bawn, Kathleen, and Michael F. Thies. 2003. "A Comparative Theory of Electoral Incentives: Representing the Unorganized under PR, Plurality, and Mixed-Member Electoral Systems." *Journal of Theoretical Politics* 15(1): 5–32.

Beck, Nathaniel. 1991. "Comparing Dynamic Specifications: The Case of Presidential Approval." *Political Analysis* 3(1): 51–87.

Beck, Nathaniel, and Jonathan N. Katz. 1995. "What to Do (and Not to Do) with Time-Series Cross-Section Data." *American Political Science Review* 89(3): 634–47.

Beck, Nathaniel, and Jonathan N. Katz. 2004. "*Time-Series-Cross-Section Issues: Dynamics, 2004.*" Paper prepared for presentation at the Summer Meeting of the Society for Political Methodology, Palo Alto, CA.

Beck, Thorsten, George Clarke, Alberto Groff, Philip Keefer, and Patrick Walsh. 2001. "New Tools in Comparative Political Economy: The Database of Political Institutions." *World Bank Economic Review* 15(1): 165–76.

Becker, Gary S. 1983. "A Theory of Competition among Pressure Groups for Political Influence." *Quarterly Journal of Economics* 98(3): 371–400.

240

Bibliography

Belassa, Bela. 1964. "The Purchasing-Power Parity Doctrine: A Reappraisal." *Journal of Political Economy* 72(6): 584–96.

Benoit, Kenneth. 2004. "Models of Electoral System Change." *Electoral Studies* 23(3): 363–89.

Beramendi, Pablo, and David Rueda. 2007. Social Democracy Constrained: Indirect Taxation in Industrial Democracies. *British Journal of Political Science* 37: 619–41.

Bergstrand, Jeffrey H. 1991. "Structural Determinants of Real Exchange Rates and National Price Levels: Some Empirical Evidence." *American Economic Review* 81(1): 325–34.

Bhagwati, Jagdish N. 1984. "Why Are Services Cheaper in the Poor Countries?" *Economic Journal* 94(June): 279–86.

Birchfield, Vicki, and Markus M. L. Crepaz. 1998. "The Impact of Constitutional Structures and Collective and Competitive Veto Points on Income Inequality in Industrialized Democracies." *European Journal of Political Research* 34(2): 175–200.

Blais, André, and Agnieszka Dobrzynska. 1998. "Turnout in Electoral Democracies." *European Journal of Political Research* 33(2): 239–62.

Blais, André, Agnieszka Dobrzynska, and Indridi Indridason. 2004. "To Adopt or Not to Adopt Proportional Representation: The Politics of Institutional Choice." *British Journal of Political Science* 35(1): 182–90.

Blomberg, S. Brock, Jeffry Frieden, and Ernesto Stein. 2005. "Sustaining Fixed Rates: The Political Economy of Currency Pegs in Latin America." *Journal of Applied Economics* 8(2): 203–25.

Boix, Carles. 1999. "Setting the Rules of the Game: The Choice of Electoral Systems in Advanced Democracies." *American Political Science Review* 93(3): 609–24.

Boix, Carles. 2003. *Democracy and Redistribution*. Cambridge: Cambridge University Press.

Bollen, Kenneth. 1993. "Liberal Democracy: Validity and Method Factors in Cross-National Measures." *American Journal of Political Science* 37(4): 1207–30.

Bull, Martin, and Gianfranco Pasquino. 2007. "A Long Quest in Vain: Institutional Reforms in Italy." *West European Politics* 30(4): 670–91.

Campbell, James E., and Steve J. Jurek. 2003. "The Decline of Competition and Change in Congressional Elections." In *The United States Congress: A Century of Change*, edited by Sunil Ahuja and Robert Dewhirst. Columbus: Ohio State University Press.

Bibliography

Casper, Gretchen and Claudiu Tufiş. 2003. "Correlation versus Interchangeability: The Limited Robustness of Empirical Finding on Democracy Using Highly Correlated Datasets." *Political Analysis* 11(2): 196–203.

Chang, Eric C. C., Miriam Golden, and Seth J. Hill. 2007. Electoral Consequences of Political Corruption. Paper delivered at the annual meeting of the American Political Science Association, 2007.

Chang, Eric C. C., Mark Kayser, and Ronald Rogowski. 2008. "Electoral Systems and Real Prices: Panel Evidence for the OECD Countries, 1970–2000." *British Journal of Political Science* 38: 739–51.

Clague, Christopher. 1986. "Determinants of the National Price Level: Some Empirical Results." *Review of Economics and Statistics* 68(2): 320–3.

Collie, Melissa, and David Brady. 1985. "The Decline of Party Voting Coalitions in the House of Representatives." In Lawrence Dodd and Bruce Oppenheimer, eds., *Congress Reconsidered*, 3rd ed., pp. 272–87. Washington, DC: CQ Press.

Colomer, Josep M., ed., 2004. *Handbook of Electoral System Choice*. New York: Palgrave MacMillan.

Cox, Gary W. 1997. *Making Votes Count: Strategic Coordination in the World's Electoral Systems*. New York: Cambridge University Press.

Cox, Gary W., and Jonathan N. Katz. 2002. *Elbridge Gerry's Salamander: The Electoral Consequences of the Reapportionment Revolution*. Cambridge: Cambridge University Press.

Cusack, Thomas R., Torben Iversen, and David Soskice. 2007. "Economic Interests and the Origins of Electoral Systems." *American Political Science Review* 101(3): 373–91.

De Boef, Suzanna, and Luke J. Keele. 2006. "Taking Time Seriously: Dynamic Regression." *American Journal of Political Science* 52: 1, 184–200.

Denzau, Arthur T., and Michael C. Munger. 1986. "Legislators and Interest Groups: How Unorganized Interests Get Represented." *American Political Science Review* 80(1): 89–106.

Diggle, Peter J., Kung-Yee Liang, and Scott L. Zeger. 1994. *Analysis of Longitudinal Data*. New York: Oxford University Press.

Djankov, Simeon, Rafael La Porta, Florencio Lopez-de-Silanes, and Andrei Shleifer. 2002. "The Regulation of Entry." *Quarterly Journal of Economics* 117(1): 1–37.

Domes, Jürgen. 1964. *Mehrheitsfraktion und Bundesregierung: Aspekte des Verhältnisse der Fraktion der CDU/CSU im zweiten und dritten Deutschen Bundestag zum Kabinett Adenauer*. Cologne: Westdeutscher Verlag.

Bibliography

Donovan, Mark. 1995. "The Politics of Electoral Reform in Italy." *International Political Science Review* 16(1): 47–64.

Downs, Anthony. 1957 [1997]. *An Economic Theory of Democracy.* New York: Addison Wesley.

Durr, Robert. 1993. "An Essay on Cointegration and Error Correction Models." *Political Analysis* 4(1): 185–228.

Duverger, Maurice. 1954. *Political Parties: Their Organization and Activity in the Modern State.* New York: Wiley.

Economist. 2005. "Structurally Unsound." November 26. http://www.economist.com/node/5164101/print

Economist. 2006a. "A logjam breaks: deregulation in Italy." August 5. http://www.economist.com/node/7258158/print

Economist 2006b. "A liberal puzzle: Italy's government." October 21. http://www.economist.com/node/8058221/print

Edwards, George. 1980. *Presidential Freedom in Congress.* San Francisco: Freeman.

Efron, Bradley, and Robert Tibshirani. 1993. *An Introduction to the Bootstrap.* Boca Raton, FL: Chapman and Hall/CRC.

Elkins, Zachary. 2000. "Gradations of Democracy? Empirical Tests of Alternative Conceptualizations." *American Journal of Political Science* 44(2): 293–300.

Engel, Charles, and John H. Rogers. 1996. "How Wide is the Border?" *American Economic Review* 86(5): 1112–25.

Engel, Charles, and John H. Rogers. 2001. "Deviations from Purchasing Power Parity: Causes and Welfare Costs." *Journal of International Economics* 55: 29–57.

Engerman, Stanley L., and Kenneth L. Sokoloff. 2002. "Factor Endowments, Inequality, and Paths of Development among New World Economies." *Economia* 3(1): 41–109.

Erikson, Robert S. 1972. "Malapportionment, Gerrymandering, and Party Fortunes in Congressional Elections." *American Political Science Review* 66(4): 1234–1335.

Esping-Andersen, Gøsta. 1990. *The Three Worlds of Welfare Capitalism.* Princeton, NJ: Princeton University Press.

Esteverz-Abé, Margarita, Torben Iversen, and David Soskice. 2001. "Social Protection and the Formation of Skills: A Re-interpretation of the Welfare State." In: Hall and Soskice 2001, chap. 4.

Feldman, Gerald. 1966. *Army, Labor, and Industry in Germany, 1914–1918.* Princeton, NJ: Princeton University Press.

Bibliography

Ferejohn, John A. 1977. "On the Decline of Competition in Congressional Elections." *American Political Science Review* 71(1): 166–76.

Fiorina, Morris P. 1977. "The Case of the Vanishing Marginals: The Bureaucracy Did It." *American Political Science Review* 71(1): 177–81.

Flora, Peter, and Arnold Heidenheimer, eds. 1981. *The Development of Welfare States in Europe and America*. New Brunswick: Transaction Books.

Franzese, Robert J., Jr. 2002. *Macroeconomic Policies of Developed Democracies*. New York: Cambridge University Press.

Gelman, Andrew, and Gary King 1990. "Estimating the Electoral Consequences of Legislative Redistricting." *Journal of the American Statistical Association* 85(410): 274–82.

Gelman, Andrew, and Gary King. 1994a. "Enhancing Democracy through Legislative Redistricting." *American Political Science Review* 88(3): 541–59.

Gelman, Andrew, and Gary King. 1994b. "A Unified Method of Evaluating Electoral Systems and Redistricting Plans." *American Journal of Political Science* 38(2): 514–54.

Gentle, James E. 2002. *Elements of Computational Statistics*, 1st edition. New York: Springer-Verlag.

Golden, Miriam A. 2004. "International Economic Sources of Regime Change: How European Economic Integration Undermined Italy's Postwar Party System." *Comparative Political Studies* 37(10): 1238–74.

Golder, Matt. 2005. "Democratic Electoral Systems around the World, 1946–2000." *Electoral Studies* 24(1): 103–21.

Gordon, Robert J., and Ian Dew-Becker. April 2008. "Controversies About the Rise of American Inequality: A Survey." National Bureau of Economic Research, Working Paper 13982. Available at: http://www.nber.org/papers/w13982. Cambridge, MA.

Green, Donald Philip, and Jonathan S. Krasno. 1988. "Salvation for the Spendthrift Incumbent: Reestimating the Effects of Campaign Spending in House Elections." *American Journal of Political Science* 32(4): 884–907.

Greene, William H. 2000. *Econometric Analysis*. Upper Saddle River, NJ: Prentice-Hall.

Griffin, John D. 2006. "Electoral Competition and Democratic Responsiveness: A Defense of the Marginality Hypothesis." *Journal of Politics* 68(4): 911–21.

Grofman, Bernard, and Arend Lijphart, eds. 1986. *Electoral Laws and Their Political Consequences*. New York: Agathon Press, Inc.

Gudgin, Graham, and Peter J. Taylor. 1979. *Seats, Votes, and the Spatial Organisation of Elections*. London: Pion Limited.

Bibliography

Hall, Peter A., and David Soskice, eds. 2001. *Varieties of Capitalism: The Institutional Foundations of Comparative Advantage*. Oxford: Oxford University Press.

Hausman, Jerry, and Ephraim Leibtag. August 2004. "CPI Bias From Supercenters: Does the BLS Know that Wal-Mart Exists?" NBER Working Paper 10712. Available at: http://www.nber.org/papers/w10712.

Hermens, Ferdinand A. 1941. *Democracy of Anarchy? A Study of Proportional Representation*. South Bend, IN: Notre Dame University Press.

Heston, Alan, Robert Summers, and Bettina Aten. October 2002. *Penn World Table*, Version 6.1. Center for International Comparisons at the University of Pennsylvania (CICUP).

Heston, Alan, Robert Summers, and Bettina Aten. September 2006. *Penn World Table*, Version 6.2, Center for International Comparisons of Production, Income, and Prices at the University of Pennsylvania.

Hirshleifer, Jack. 1991. "The Paradox of Power." *Economics and Politics* 3: 177–200.

Hiwatari, Nobuhiro. 2001a. "Electoral Reforms and the Policy Predicaments of Parliamentary Governments under Global Capital Mobility." Institute of Social Sciences, University of Tokyo. Available at: http://www.iss.u-tokyo.ac.jp/~hiwatari/papers/010801.pdf (March 6, 2008).

Hiwatari, Nobuhiro. 2001b. "Why Electoral Reform and Party System Reorganization? The Impact of Global Capital Mobility on the Consensus Democratic Institutions of Italy and Japan." Institute of Social Sciences, University of Tokyo. Available at: http://web.iss.u-tokyo.ac.jp/~hiwatari/papers/010802.pdf (March 6, 2008).

Ho, Daniel. 2003. "Majoritarian Electoral Systems and Consumer Power: A Matching Rejoinder." Paper prepared for presentation at the Summer Meeting of the Society for Political Methodology, Minneapolis, MN.

Honaker, James, Gary King, and Matthew Blackwell. 2010. "Amelia II: A Program for Missing Data." http://gking.harvard.edu/amelia/.

Huber, John D., and G. Bingham Powell, Jr. 1994. "Congruence between Citizens and Policymakers in Two Visions of Liberal Democracy." *World Politics* 46(3): 291–326.

Huntington, Samuel P. 1968. *Political Order in Changing Societies*. New Haven, CT: Yale University Press.

International Monetary Fund. April 2002. World Economic Outlook Database, World Economic and Financial Surveys. Available at: http://www.imf.org/external/pubs/ft/weo/2002/01/data.

Bibliography

Iversen, Torben, and David Soskice. 2006. "Electoral Systems and the Politics of Coalitions: Why Some Democracies Redistribute More Than Others." *American Political Science Review* 100: 165–82.

Iversen, Torben, and David Soskice. 2009. An Institutional Model of Real Exchange Rates and Competititiveness. Forthcoming, *American Political Science Review*, 2010. Available at: www.people.fas.harvard.edu/~iversen/index_files/page0006.htm.

Jacobson, Gary C. 1987. "The Marginals Never Vanished: Incumbency Advantage and Competition in Elections to the U.S. House of Representatives, 1952–1982." *American Journal of Political Science* 31: 126–41.

Katz, Richard S. 1981. *A Theory of Parties and Electoral Systems.* Baltimore, MD: Johns Hopkins University Press.

Katz, Richard S. 1997. *Democracy and Elections.* Oxford: Oxford University Press.

Katz, Richard S. 2006. "Electoral Reform in Italy: Expectations and Results." *Acta Politica* 41(3): 285.

Katzenstein, Peter. 1985. *Small States in World Markets: Industrial Policy in Europe.* Ithaca, NY: Cornell University Press.

Kayser, Mark Andreas. 2004. "The Price-Level Effect of Electoral Competitiveness." Paper presented at the Annual Meeting of the American Political Science Association.

Kayser, Mark Andreas, and Drew Linzer. 2008. "Electoral Competitiveness: Toward a Universal Measure." Paper presented at the Annual Meeting of the American Political Science Association. Available at: http://mail.rochester.edu/~mksr/papers/KL-Compet-080726.pdf.

Keefer, Philip, and David Stasavage. 2003. "The Limits of Delegation, Veto Players, Central Bank Independence, and the Credibility of Monetary Policy." *American Political Science Review* 97(3): 407–23.

Kendall M.G., and A. Stuart. 1950. "Cubic Proportion in Electoral Results." *British Journal of Sociology* 1: 183–97.

Keesing's World News Archive. Available at: www.keesings.com.

King, Gary. 1989. "Representation through Legislative Redistricting: A Stochastic Model." *American Journal of Political Science* 33(4): 787–824.

King, Gary. 1990. "Electoral Responsiveness and Partisan Bias in Multiparty Democracies." *Legislative Studies Quarterly* 15(2): 159–81.

King, Gary, and Robert X. Browning. 1987. "Democratic Representation and Partisan Bias in Congressional Elections." *American Political Science Review* 81(4): 1251–73.

Bibliography

King, Gary, James Honaker, Anne Joseph, and Kenneth Scheve. 2001. "Analyzing Incomplete Political Science Data: An Alternative Algorithm for Multiple Imputation." *American Political Science Review* 95(1): 49–69.

Kitschelt, Herbert, and Steven I. Wilkinson, eds. 2006. *Patrons, Clients, and Policies: Patterns of Democratic Accountability and Political Competition.* Cambridge: Cambridge University Press.

Kittel, Bernhard, and Hannes Winner. 2005. "How Reliable is Pooled Analysis in Political Economy? The Globalization-Welfare State Nexus Revisited." *European Journal of Political Research* 44(2): 269–93.

Kravis, Irving B., and Robert E. Lipsey. 1983. "Toward an Explanation of National Price Levels." *Princeton Studies in International Finance*, No. 52. Princeton, NJ: Princeton University Press.

Kravis, Irving B., and Robert E. Lipsey. 1988. "National Price Levels and the Prices of Tradables and Nontradables." *American Economic Review* 78(2): 474–8.

Krugman, Paul. 1987. "Pricing to Market When the Exchange Rate Changes." In *Real-Financial Linkages among Open Economies*, Sven W. Arndt and J. David Richardson, eds. Cambridge, MA: MIT Press.

Kunicova, Jana, and Susan Rose-Ackerman. 2005. "Electoral Rules and Constitutional Structures as Constraints on Corruption." *British Journal of Political Science* 35: 573–606.

Lee, Jong-Wha. 1993. "International Trade, Distortions, and Long-Run Economic Growth." *IMF Staff Papers* 40(2): 299–328.

Lewis, William W. 2004. *The Power of Productivity: Wealth, Poverty, and the Threat to Global Stability.* Chicago: University of Chicago Press.

Liang, Kung-Yee, and Scott L. Zeger. 1986. "Longitudinal Data Analysis Using Generalized Linear Models." *Biometrika* 73(1): 13–22.

Lijphart, Arend. 1994. *Electoral Systems and Party Systems: A Study of Twenty-Seven Democracies, 1945–1990.* New York: Oxford University Press.

Lijphart, Arend. 1999. *Patterns of Democracy: Government Forms and Performance in Thirty-Six Countries.* New Haven, CT: Yale University Press.

Lindert, Peter H. 2003. "Why the Welfare State Looks Like a Free Lunch." NBER Working Paper 9869.

Lipton, Michael. 1977. *Why Poor People Stay Poor: Urban Bias in World Development.* Cambridge, MA: Harvard University Press.

Lizzeri, Alessandro, and Nicola Persico. 2001. "The Provision of Public Goods under Alternative Electoral Incentives." *American Economic Review* 91(1): 225–39.

Bibliography

Mauro, Paolo. 1995. "Corruption and Growth." *Quarterly Journal of Economics* 110(3): 681–712.

Mayhew, David R. 1974. "Congressional Elections: The Case of the Vanishing Marginals." *Polity* 6: 295–317.

McDonald, Michael D., Silvia M. Mendes, and Ian Budge. 2004. "What Are Elections For? Conferring the Median Mandate." *British Journal of Political Science* 34(1): 1–26.

Meltzer, Allan H., and Scott F. Richard. 1981. "A Rational Theory of the Size of Government." *Journal of Political Economy* 89(5): 914–27.

Milesi-Ferretti, Gian Maria, Roberto Perotti, and Massimo Rostagno. 2002. "Electoral Systems and Public Spending." *Quarterly Journal of Economics* 117(2): 609–57.

Monroe, Burt L. 1998. "Bias and Responsiveness in Multiparty and Multigroup Representation." Paper presented at the Political Methodology Summer Meeting, University of California at San Diego.

Mossberg, Walter. 2007. "Free My Phone." *All Things Digital*, October 21. Available at: http://mossblog.allthingsd.com/20071021/free-my-phone.

Munck, Gerardo, and Jay Verkuilen. 2005. "Research Designs." In Kimberly Kempf-Leonard (ed.) *Encyclopedia of Social Measurement*, vol. 3 pp. 385–95. San Diego, CA.: Academic Press.

Nadeau, Richard, Richard G. Niemi, and Antoine Yoshinaka. 2002. "A Cross-National Analysis of Economic Voting: Taking Account of the Political Context across Time and Nations." *Electoral Studies* 21(3): 403–23.

Neyman, J., and Elizabeth L. Scott. 1948. "Consistent Estimates Based on Partially Consistent Observations." *Econometrica* 16(1): 1–32.

Organization for Economic Co-Operation and Development (OECD). 2002. OECD Health Data. Summarized at www.oecd.org/pdf/M00031000/M00031130.pdf.

OECD 1999. *Economic Survey of Italy*. Paris: OECD Publishing.

OECD. 2000. *Italy – The Role of Competition Policy in Regulatory Reform*. OECD Regulatory Reform Program Report.

OECD. 2001a. OECD Reviews of Regulatory Reform: Regulatory Reform in Italy. Paris: OECD Publishing. ISBN: 9789264186606 (March).

OECD. 2001b. Regulatory Reform in Italy: Government Capacity to Assure Quality Regulation. Prepared in support for OECD Review of Regulatory Reform in Italy (2001).

OECD. 2001c. The New Economy: Beyond the Hype: *The OECD Growth Project*. Paris: OECD Publishing.

Bibliography

OECD. 2002. OECD Economic Surveys – Italy: Structural Reforms to Raise Potential Growth.

OECD. 2007. OECD Reviews of Regulatory Reform: Italy. Ensuring Regulatory Quality Across Levels of Government. OECD Publishing (also see Executive Summary).

O'Rourke, Kevin H., and Jeffrey G. Williamson. 1999. *Globalization and History: The Evolution of a Nineteenth-Century Atlantic Economy.* Cambridge, MA: MIT Press.

Pagano, Marco, and Paolo F. Volpin. 2005. "The Political Economy of Corporate Governance." *American Economic Review* 95(4): 1005–30.

Paldam, Martin. 1991. "How Robust is the Vote Function? A Study of Seventeen Nations over Four Decades." In *Economics and Politics: The Calculus of Support,* Helmut Norpoth, Michael Lewis-Beck, and Jean Dominique Lafay, eds. Ann Arbor: University of Michigan Press, 9–32.

Peltzman, Sam. 1976. "Toward a More General Theory of Regulation." *Journal of Law and Economics* 19(2): 211–40.

Persson, Torsten, and Guido Tabellini. 2000. *Political Economics: Explaining Economic Policy.* Cambridge, MA: MIT Press.

Persson, Torsten, and Guido Tabellini. 2003. *The Economic Effects of Constitutions.* Cambridge, MA: MIT Press.

Persson, Torsten, and Guido Tabellini. 2004. "Constitutional Rules and Fiscal Policy Outcomes." *American Economic Review* 94(1): 25–45.

Pigou, Arthur C. 1938. *The Economics of Welfare,* 4th ed. London: Macmillan and Co.

Powell, G. Bingham, Jr. 1982. *Contemporary Democracies: Participation, Stability, and Violence.* Cambridge, MA: Harvard University Press.

Powell, G. Bingham, Jr. 2000. *Elections as Instruments of Democracy: Majoritarian and Proportional Visions.* New Haven, CT: Yale University Press.

Powell, G. Bingham, Jr. 2002. "PR, the Median Voter, and Economic Policy: An Exploration." Paper prepared for presentation at the Annual Meeting of the American Political Science Association, Boston, MA.

Powell, G. Bingham, Jr., and Guy D. Whitten. 1993. "A Cross-National Analysis of Economic Voting: Taking Account of the Political Context." *American Journal of Political Science* 73(2): 391–414.

Przeworski, Adam, Michael E. Alvarez, Jose Antonio Cheibub, and Fernando Limongi. 2000. *Democracy and Development: Political Institutions and Well-Being in the World, 1950–1990.* New York: Cambridge University Press.

Quitzau, Jörn. 2002. "Is Germany Heading the Same Way as Japan?" Frankfurt Voice, Deutsche Bank Research, July 9.

Bibliography

Rae, Douglas. 1971. *The Political Consequences of Electoral Laws*. New Haven, CT: Yale University Press.

Rafael Reuveny, and Quan Li. 2003. "Economic Openness, Democracy, and Income Inequality: An Empirical Analysis" *Comparative Political Studies*, 36(5): 575–601.

Rauch, James E. 1995. "Bureaucracy, Infrastructure, and Economic Growth: Evidence from U.S. Cities During the Progressive Era." *American Economic Review* 85: 968–79.

Rogoff, Kenneth. 1996. "The Purchasing Power Parity Puzzle." *Journal of Economic Literature* 34(2): 647–68.

Rogowski, Ronald, Eric C. C. Chang, and Mark Andreas Kayser. 2004. "Electoral Systems and Real Prices: Panel Evidence for the OECD Countries, 1970–2000." Paper prepared for presentation at the Annual Meeting of the American Political Science Association, Chicago, IL.

Rogowski, Ronald, and Mark Andreas Kayser. 2002. "Majoritarian Electoral Systems and Consumer Power: Price-Level Evidence from the OECD Countries." *American Journal of Political Science* 46(3): 526–39.

Rogowski, Ronald, and Duncan Macrae. 2008. Inequality and Institutions: What Theory, History, and (Some) Data Tell Us. In: Pablo Beramendi and Christopher Anderson, eds., *Democracy, Inequality and Representation: A Comparative Perspective*, chap. 11. New York: Russell Sage Foundation.

Rosenbluth, Frances McCall. 1996. "Institutionalization and Electoral Politics in Japan." In *Internationalization and Domestic Politics*, Robert O. Keohane and Helen V. Milner, eds. Cambridge: Cambridge University Press, 137–58.

Rosenbluth, Frances and Ross Schaap. 2003. "The Domestic Politics of Banking Regulation." *International Organization* 57(Spring): 307–36.

Roubini, Nouriel, and Jeffrey D. Sachs. 1989. "Political and Economic Determinants of Budget Deficits in Industrial Democracies." *European Economic Review* 33(5): 903–33.

Rueda, David. 2005. "Insider-Outsider Politics in Industrialized Democracies: The Challenge to Social Democratic Parties." *American Political Science Review* 99(1): 61–74.

Rueda, David. 2006. "Social Democracy and Active Labour Market Policies: Insiders, Outsiders, and the Politics of Employment Promotion." *British Journal of Political Science* 36(3): 385–406.

Rueda, David. 2007. *Social Democracy Inside Out: Government Partisanship, Insiders, and Outsiders in Industrialized Democracies*. Oxford: Oxford University Press.

Bibliography

Samuelson, Paul A. 1964. "Theoretical Notes on Trade Problems." *Review of Economics and Statistics* 46(2): 145–54.

Scalapino, Robert A., and Junosuke Massumi. 1962. *Parties and Politics in Contemporary Japan.* Berkeley and Los Angeles: University of California Press.

Scartascini, Carlos. 2002. "Political Institutions and Regulation: An Inquiry on the Impact of Electoral Systems on the Regulation of Entry." Working Paper, Inter-American Development Bank.

Stigler, George J. 1971. "The Theory of Economic Regulation." *Bell Journal of Economics and Management Science* 2(1): 3–21.

Taagepera, Rein, and Matthew Soberg Shugart. 1989. *Seats and Votes: The Effects and Determinants of Electoral Systems.* New Haven, CT: Yale University Press.

Tavits, Margit. 2004. "The Size of Government in Majoritarian and Consensus Democracies." *Comparative Political Studies* 37(3): 340–59.

Tavits, Margit. 2005. "The Development of Stable Party Support: Electoral Dynamics in Post-Communist Europe." *American Journal of Political Science* 49(2): 283–98.

Tavits, Margit. 2007. Clarity of Responsibility and Corruption. *American Journal of Political Science* 51: 218.

Theil, Henri. 1969. "The Desired Political Entropy." *American Political Science Review* 63: 521–25.

Thelen, Kathleen. 2004. *How Institutions Evolve: The Political Economy of Skills in Germany, Britain, the United States, and Japan.* Cambridge: Cambridge University Press.

Ticchi, Davide, and Andrea Vindigni. 2010. "Endogenous Constitutions." *Economic Journal* 120(543): 1–39.

Treier, Shawn, and Simon Jackman. 2003. "Democracy as a Latent Variable." Paper prepared for presentation at the Summer Meeting of the Society for Political Methodology, Minneapolis, MN.

Treisman, Daniel. 2000. "The Causes of Corruption: A Cross-National Study." *Journal of Public Economics* 76(3): 399–457.

Tufte, Edward R. 1973. The Relationship between Seats and Votes in Two-Party Systems. *American Political Science Review* 67(2): 540–54.

Vanhanen, Tatu. 1997. *Prospects of Democracy: A Study of 172 Countries.* New York: Routledge.

Varian, Hal R. 1992. *Microeconomic Analysis,* 3rd ed. New York and London: W. W. Norton & Co.

Bibliography

Vassallo, Salvatore. 2007. "Government under Berlusconi: The Functioning of the Core Institutions in Italy." *West European Politics* 30(4): 692–710.

Verdier, Daniel. 2001. "Capital Mobility and the Origins of Stock Markets." *International Organization* 55: 327–56.

Verdier, Daniel. 2002. *Moving Money: Banking and Finance in the Industrialized World.* Cambridge: Cambridge University Press.

Vernby, Kare. 2007. "Strikes are More Common in Countries with Majoritarian Electoral Systems." *Public Choice* 132: 65–84.

Visco, Vincenzo. 2002. "Budget Consolidation and Economic Reform in Italy." Working Paper. Oxford University.

von Beyme, Klaus. 1985. *Political Parties in Western Democracies.* Aldershot: Gower.

Walker, Marcus. 2004. "Behind Slow Growth in Europe: Citizens' Tight Grip on Wallets." *Wall Street Journal,* December 10, Section A, p. 1.

Wallerstein, Michael. 1989. "Union Organization in Advanced Industrial Democracies." *American Political Science Review* 83(2): 481–501.

Wawro, Gregory. 2002. "Estimating Dynamic Panel Data Models in Political Science." *Political Analysis* 10(1): 25–48.

Whitten, Guy D., and Harvey D. Palmer. 1999. "Cross-National Analyses of Economic Voting." *Electoral Studies* 18(1): 49–67.

World Bank. 2005. World Development Indicators Online. Available at: http://devdata.worldbank.org/dataonline.

Zaller, John. 1998. "Politicians as Prize Fighters: Electoral Selection and Incumbency Advantage." In: *Politicians and Party Politics,* John G. Geer, ed., Baltimore: Johns Hopkins University Press.

Zorn, Christopher J. W. 2001. "Generalized Estimating Equation Models for Correlated Data: A Review with Applications." *American Journal of Political Science* 45(2): 470–90.

Index

Index

Index

Index

Index

Index

Index

Index

Index

Index

Robert O. Keohane and Helen B. Milner, eds., *Internationalization and Domestic Politics*

Herbert Kitschelt, *The Transformation of European Social Democracy*

Herbert Kitschelt, Kirk A. Hawkins, Juan Pablo Luna, Guillermo Rosas, and Elizabeth J. Zechmeister, *Latin American Party Systems*

Herbert Kitschelt, Peter Lange, Gary Marks, and John D. Stephens, eds., *Continuity and Change in Contemporary Capitalism*

Herbert Kitschelt, Zdenka Mansfeldova, Radek Markowski, and Gabor Toka, *Post-Communist Party Systems*

David Knoke, Franz Urban Pappi, Jeffrey Broadbent, and Yutaka Tsujinaka, eds., *Comparing Policy Networks*

Allan Kornberg and Harold D. Clarke, *Citizens and Community: Political Support in a Representative Democracy*

Amie Kreppel, *The European Parliament and the Supranational Party System*

David D. Laitin, *Language Repertoires and State Construction in Africa*

Fabrice E. Lehoucq and Ivan Molina, *Stuffing the Ballot Box: Fraud, Electoral Reform, and Democratization in Costa Rica*

Mark Irving Lichbach and Alan S. Zuckerman, eds., *Comparative Politics: Rationality, Culture, and Structure, second edition*

Evan Lieberman, *Race and Regionalism in the Politics of Taxation in Brazil and South Africa*

Pauline Jones Luong, *Institutional Change and Political Continuity in Post-Soviet Central Asia*

Julia Lynch, *Age in the Welfare State: The Origins of Social Spending on Pensioners, Workers, and Children*

Beatriz Magaloni, *Voting for Autocracy: Hegemonic Party Survival and its Demise in Mexico*

James Mahoney, *Colonialism and Postcolonial Development: Spanish America in Comparative Perspective*

James Mahoney and Dietrich Rueschemeyer, eds., *Historical Analysis and the Social Sciences*

Scott Mainwaring and Matthew Soberg Shugart, eds., *Presidentialism and Democracy in Latin America*

Isabela Mares, *The Politics of Social Risk: Business and Welfare State Development*

Isabela Mares, *Taxation, Wage Bargaining, and Unemployment*

Anthony W. Marx, *Making Race, Making Nations: A Comparison of South Africa, the United States, and Brazil*

Doug McAdam, John McCarthy, and Mayer Zald, eds., *Comparative Perspectives on Social Movements*

Bonnie Meguid, *Party Competition between Unequals: Strategies and Electoral Fortunes in Western Europe*

Joel S. Migdal, *State in Society: Studying How States and Societies Constitute One Another*

Joel S. Migdal, Atul Kohli, and Vivienne Shue, eds., *State Power and Social Forces: Domination and Transformation in the Third World*

Scott Morgenstern and Benito Nacif, eds., *Legislative Politics in Latin America*

Layna Mosley, *Global Capital and National Governments*

Wolfgang C. Müller and Kaare Strøm, *Policy, Office, or Votes?*

Maria Victoria Murillo, *Labor Unions, Partisan Coalitions, and Market Reforms in Latin America*

Maria Victoria Murillo, *Political Competition, Partisanship, and Policy Making in Latin American Public Utilities*

Ton Notermans, *Money, Markets, and the State: Social Democratic Economic Policies since 1918*